Authors, Agents, and Publishers (

Authors

"I've known Fauzia for over twenty years, and I can honestly say that no one knows more about the ins and outs of online marketing for books. Fauzia gives authors the practical advice they need to find as wide an audience as possible for their books."
—**R. J. Palacio, author of the *New York Times* bestseller *Wonder***

"Fauzia Burke is intelligent, well connected, and effective. She knows how to reach the parts of the media that conventional PR either doesn't understand or wrongly ignores."
—**Charles Spencer, author of *Killers of the King***

"In these days, an author needs a steady, capable guide to navigate the many difficulties of getting books seen and heard. Fauzia's approach works, and the steps she has outlined in her book will help any author build a base of readers. She's simply the best."
—**Jan Jarboe Russell, author of the *New York Times* bestseller *The Train to Crystal City***

"Fauzia's creativity and diligent commitment to online publicity and social media are unsurpassed. Unequivocally, she is the premier go-to online marketer."
—**Bill Bradley, former US Senator and author of *We Can All Do Better***

"What author isn't intimidated by the complexities and nuances of online marketing? Anyone who has worked with Fauzia Burke! This book reflects the wisdom gained from years of painstakingly navigating the digital labyrinth on behalf of her clients."
—**Larry J. Sabato, Director, University of Virginia Center for Politics, and author of *The Kennedy Half Century***

Publishers

"Fauzia Burke was talking about online marketing years before the rest of us even knew what that meant, and she continues to lead the way. We should consider ourselves lucky that she is as generous in sharing her hard-won knowledge as she is ahead of the curve in gaining it."
—**Bob Miller, President and Publisher, Flatiron Books/Macmillan**

"Always innovative and effective. I have no reservations in recommending Fauzia Burke."

—**Judith Curr, President and Publisher, Atria Publishing Group/Simon & Schuster**

"Fauzia Burke knows better than anyone how to utilize the broad and sometimes confusing array of digital marketing tools on behalf of books."

—**Walter Weintz, former Chief Marketing and Sales Officer, Workman Publishing**

"Fauzia Burke is one of the most innovative marketing experts in the publishing industry. She brings positive, pragmatic, and powerful expertise to any author's table."

—**Kate Rados, Director, Community Development, The Crown Publishing Group, Penguin Random House**

Agents

"When it comes to publicizing a book on the web, nobody has the range and expertise of Fauzia Burke."

—**Larry J. Kirshbaum, literary agent, Waxman Leavell Literary Agency**

"Fauzia Burke is an industry leader in the world of online publicity and marketing. I have recommended Fauzia to many clients, with total confidence, and they have all been thrilled with the results."

—**Wendy Sherman, literary agent and founder of Wendy Sherman Associates**

"Armed with years of experience, Fauzia has been successfully pioneering the world of online marketing to help authors connect with their readers and produce terrific, long-lasting results."

—**Amy Hughes, literary agent, Dunow, Carlson & Lerner Literary Agency**

Fauzia Burke has promoted the books of the following authors, among many others:

Alan Alda

Arianna Huffington

Arthur Agatston, M.D.

Atul Gawande

Barbara Delinsky

Barbara Ehrenreich

Brian Tracy

Carmine Gallo

Claire Shipman

Daniel G. Amen, M.D.

Daniel Silva

Darren Hardy

Dean Koontz

Deepak Chopra, M.D.

Doug Stanton

Dr. Larry J. Sabato

Elizabeth Edwards

Evan Handler

Frances Mayes

Greg Behrendt

Jacqueline Winspear

Jan Jarboe Russell

Jeffrey Archer

Joe Pantoliano

Kathy Freston

Katty Kay

Kim Edwards

Lee and Bob Woodruff

Lidia Bastianich

Lisa Bloom

Liz Vaccariello

LL Cool J

Lord Charles Spencer

Mallika Chopra

Maria Shriver

Marina Keegan

Marlo Thomas

Masaru Emoto

Mayo Clinic

Melissa Francis

Mika Brzezinski

Mohsin Hamid

Mollie Katzen

Reza Aslan

Richard A. Clarke

Rick Atkinson

Ron Clark

Rory Stewart

S. C. Gwynne

Salman Rushdie

Sandra Lee

Scott Turow

Seth Godin

Sue Grafton

Tana French

Ted Kerasote

Temple Grandin

Tom Brokaw

Tom Wolfe

Tosca Reno

Tracy Chevalier

Vincent Bugliosi

Online Marketing
for
Busy Authors

Online Marketing
for
Busy Authors

A Step-by-Step Guide

Fauzia Burke

Berrett–Koehler Publishers, Inc.
a BK Life book

Berrett-Koehler Publishers, Inc.
1333 Broadway, Suite 1000
Oakland, CA 94612
Tel: (510) 817-2277   Fax: (510) 817-2278   www.bkconnection.com

Ordering Information
Quantity sales. Special discounts are available on quantity purchases by corporations, associations, and others. For details, contact the Special Sales Department at the Berrett-Koehler address above.

Individual sales. Berrett-Koehler publications are available through most bookstores. They can also be ordered directly from Berrett-Koehler: Tel: (800) 929-2929; Fax: (802) 864-7626; www.bkconnection.com

Orders for college textbook/course adoption use. Please contact Berrett-Koehler: Tel: (800) 929-2929; Fax: (802) 864-7626.

Orders by U.S. trade bookstores and wholesalers. Please contact Ingram Publisher Services: Tel: (800) 509-4887; Fax: (800) 838-1149; E-mail: customer.service @ingrampublisherservices.com; or visit www.ingrampublisherservices.com /Ordering for details about electronic ordering.

Berrett-Koehler and the BK logo are registered trademarks of Berrett-Koehler Publishers, Inc.

Printed in the United States of America

Berrett-Koehler books are printed on long-lasting acid-free paper. When it is available, we choose paper that has been manufactured by environmentally responsible processes. These may include using trees grown in sustainable forests, incorporating recycled paper, minimizing chlorine in bleaching, or recycling the energy produced at the paper mill.

Library of Congress Cataloging-in-Publication Data

Names: Burke, Fauzia, author.
Title: Online marketing for busy authors : a step-by-step guide / Fauzia Burke.
Description: San Francisco : Berrett-Koehler Publishers, [2016] | Includes index.
Identifiers: LCCN 2015049358 | ISBN 978-1-62656-785-6 (pbk.)
Subjects: Books--Internet marketing. | Authorship--Internet marketing.
Classification: LCC Z285.6 .B87 2016 | DDC 070.5/2--dc23
LC record available at http://lccn.loc.gov/2015049358

FIRST EDITION

20 19 18 17 16   10 9 8 7 6 5 4 3 2 1

Cover design by Bradford Foltz
Book design and production by Steven Hiatt/Hiatt & Dragon, San Francisco
Copyediting by Steven Hiatt
Proofreading by Tom Hassett

Dedicated to my mother, Nuzhat Subhani,
for her unyielding support and her
unconditional love

Contents

Foreword *by S.C. Gwynne*   ix

Introduction   1

Phase 1: Getting Organized   5

  1 Personal Branding 101   7

  2 You Gotta Dream Big   15

  3 Know Thy Reader   19

  4 Get Real With Your Goals   27

  5 Best Advice in the Business   35

  6 Your Priority List   41

Phase 2: Turning Your Thinking Into Action   49

  7 Your Online Marketing Plan   51

  8 Building Your Website   61

  9 Mailing List of Fans   73

 10 To Blog or Not to Blog   79

 11 Social Media and Social Networking   91

 12 DIY Online Book Publicity   111

Phase 3: Staying the Course   125

13   Promote Without Being Promotional   127

14   Monitor and Adjust   133

Some Parting Advice   139

Acknowledgments   143

Index   145

About the Author   149

Foreword

by S.C. Gwynne

I come from the old world of publishing, a place where it is considered smart marketing to send an author on a tour to a chain bookstore in Kansas City, where he sits in a corner and signs a few books for passersby. A world where publicity consists of sending review copies of your book to newspaper editors, where they take their place among the 200 other books that hit the editor's desk that week. Maybe those editors get a follow-up call. Maybe they don't.

I lived in this world for a long time. Like so many other authors, I found myself in a sort of prison of limited access. The world was a very big place, but the opportunities to promote your book were severely limited. There was nothing you could do. Everyone complained about it.

Then I met Fauzia Burke and everything changed. At the time I was not completely naïve about things digital. I maintained a website, used the Internet in my own work, and had a

Facebook page. What I did not have was any understanding of how to promote my books online.

When I published my most recent book, *Rebel Yell: The Violence, Passion, and Redemption of Stonewall Jackson*, I engaged her company, FSB Associates, to help me in three areas: building a website, marketing my book through social media, and doing online publicity. The first thing FSB did was to establish a close link with my publisher, Scribner. From then on they worked closely to balance Scribner's more traditional marketing with their online efforts. From my point of view, it was as though Scribner had just acquired an online arm. My publicists at Scribner saw it that way, too. They loved working with FSB.

What FSB did, very quickly and very thoroughly, was a steep dive into the digital world. As it turned out, they knew this world very well, the product of many years of working with online editors. They solicited, and got, dozens of reviews on blogs and websites, many of them extremely prominent ones. They pitched each editor individually: no shotgun blasts. They solicited, and got, writing contracts for me, actual writing gigs at various blogs. They got me speaking engagements. They pushed very hard. One of their "target" lists alone had more than 100 websites—and they were the right ones, too. They sent me regular updates showing me what they had done. It was amazing to watch it all unfold.

So instead of sitting in that Kansas City Barnes & Noble cooling my heels, I was being reviewed in the Huffington Post, The Daily Beast, and the Washington Independent Review of Books. I was writing columns for the History News Network and *The American Legion*. I was suddenly living in this other world. That world also included Facebook and Twitter, where FSB took me from a passive bystander to an active participant. All of what they did was quantified and delivered in precise metrics in regular reports. I always knew exactly what they were doing and how well it was working. Behind it all stood my glittering new website, a place to drive traffic and build audience.

Fauzia's work had a lot to with making *Rebel Yell* a *New York Times* national bestseller. She opened the door to this new world for me. And, as I tell my author friends, once you have seen that world you are never going back. The book that follows is a wonderful distillation of all the knowledge she has gained while revolutionizing the field of online literary marketing. I recommend it!

S.C. Gwynne

Author of two *New York Times* bestsellers,
Empire of the Summer Moon and *Rebel Yell*

Introduction

In my twenty years of promoting books online, I have worked with bestselling authors, celebrity authors, longtime authors, first-time authors, and some self-published authors. While the challenges may differ from book to book, all authors have a similar concern: how to spend their time effectively promoting their book and expanding their brands online while writing the best book possible. Whether you're writing your first book or you write three books a year, you are probably very busy and you must make every minute count.

Together, we will figure out the best use of your time and the best way to engage with your specific readers. I hope to make the marketing process meaningful and fun for you. I am not going to tell you that if you follow my advice, your book will be #1 on Amazon (that would be a great sales pitch, though), but what I can tell you is that if you follow my advice, you will create meaningful interactions with your readers and build a long-term, successful personal brand online. Having visibility online is not just about selling a book, it's about building a career.

I have written this book to help you do just that. I think it would be helpful for you to read this book once in its entirety before doing the actual worksheets. It will give you the big picture before you take the deep dive. This is an introductory book with a strategic look at online marketing for authors. There is a lot of information to absorb here, so I have made the book interactive. You'll find worksheets and checklists, as well as bulleted lists, tips, quotes, and advice from book publishing professionals, throughout the book.

Some of the information in the book is available on the web and even in my own blogs, but I find that having a clear road map is really important so you don't spend a lot of time chasing down information without having a plan to implement the ideas. I've organized the book in three phases to help you digest a process that feels overwhelming to most authors. In the first phase, we dig right into understanding what personal branding is and why it is important for you. We work on your motivations, dreams, and goals, and on understanding your readers. This is an important step, because it will help you make choices about where to spend your valuable time. We end with a priority list in chapter 6. This list does not have the coolest options (such as the newest video creation tool), but it does have the options that have produced the best results for my clients.

In phase 2 of the book, we'll focus on turning your priorities into action. Because it can take a couple of years to see the fruits of your labor, we work on creating a sustainable online marketing plan. I offer advice on designing a successful website, on building a mailing list of Super Fans, on blogging, and on creating an engagement strategy for social media. I also cover DIY online publicity tips and ideas you can use to create visibility for your book. All of these activities will help you establish a strong digital footprint and online brand.

Phase 3 is called Staying the Course and offers tips and ideas to continue this work without feeling the burnout experienced by many authors. One of the key concerns that my clients share is what to post on social media. By the end of the book you should not only know what to post but when and where as well.

The old saying that you can't be all things to all people is more true today than ever. Be a specialist as you build your community. There is only one *you*! Your online brand will serve you in everything you do, and it will help you in magical ways by opening doors to unexpected opportunities. It has done that for me, and for many of my clients. I can't wait to hear how this work helps you.

Phase 1
Getting Organized

Chapter 1

Personal Branding 101

All of us need to understand the importance of branding. We are CEOs of our own companies: Me Inc.
Tom Peters

When I ask authors how they feel about online marketing, the answer I get most often is, "I feel overwhelmed." I understand that feeling, but it doesn't have to be that way.

There has never been a better time to be an author, because for the first time authors have direct access to their readers. While there is more competition in the marketplace, there is also more opportunity.

The biggest challenge for most of my clients is finding the time to build their brands and market their books while writing the best book possible. To thrive in today's competitive markets, personal branding is more important than ever. Your ability to successfully execute your online marketing plan will help you capture and hold your reader's attention.

By reading this book you will have already taken the first step toward accepting your role as the marketing director of your career. You can begin your online marketing work as soon as you have an idea for your book. You will find that it is easier to get an agent and/or a publisher and certainly easier to build your audience if you have already built a personal brand online.

When readers identify with you and your brand, they feel loyal and connected to you. It is important to respect this loyalty and make sure you are providing the best information possible. For every author, building a relationship with readers should be a top goal (after making sure the book is the best that it can be). By identifying your ideal audience and reaching out to them, you will be building connections with your readers. As marketing expert and author Seth Godin says, "Make a dent in the conversation among your chosen audience. As more people talk about your book, the more people will be buying your book." He's got that right.

With social media, readers and authors can connect like never before. Google searches, micro-communities, and niche marketing give authors unprecedented access to their readers. There was a time when authors could only guess about the people who read their books. Today, authors can not only know their readers, they can be friends with them.

Readers today are tech savvy and resourceful. They know how to get the information they need, and they have high expectations from authors. They don't just expect a new book, they expect a community along with their book. You'll need to evolve your marketing to accommodate this new kind of reader: a reader whose loyalty you can have—once you have earned it. Is that too much to expect? Perhaps. But this is your new reader, and she will stay with you if you stay with her.

Many successful authors have done an enviable job of branding themselves and their work and building reader communities around their books. Their brands are so commonly known they can be described in a word—marketing, vegan, wellness, yoga, entrepreneurship, leadership. You may not have read their books, but you know what they publish. Their communities trust them. People who share their point of view flock to their sites. If your audience can effectively describe you and your message in a word, you have established a clear, powerful brand.

 Tip for #BusyAuthors

If you don't invest in your brand, no one else will either.

What is your online brand?

The best part about online marketing is that it levels the playing field. We are more connected than ever before so the author with the biggest marketing budget doesn't always win. Although establishing your brand takes time and consistent effort, the world of social media can speed up the process of creating connections. Yet with all this interconnectedness, how do you prevent your brand from getting lost in all the social media noise?

The answer: Be uniquely you. Aim for authenticity. Take some time to consider what you want people to think of when they think of you.

Every year I attend a branding conference at Columbia University called Brite. I love Brite because it gives me a chance to step outside the book publishing industry and hear success stories from other industries.

A couple of years ago, I heard a presentation from Mary Beech, chief marketing officer of Kate Spade. I was so impressed with their branding mission and how clearly they knew the "Kate Spade girl." She said that "without a clear brand voice, social media can be paralyzing and downright detrimental." I agree.

It is important to make your brand as clear and compelling as possible. If you had to go around a room and describe your brand to a group of people, could you do it in just a few sentences? You want people to gravitate toward you because they identify with your brand, so keep it impactful and interesting. Here are some questions that can help you think about your personal brand.

 Tip for #BusyAuthors

A personal brand statement allows you to carve out your niche and helps you decide the content and tone of what you share.

Questions to help you identify your brand

As you answer these questions, remember that this is not an elevator pitch. You don't have to share these responses with anyone. It's just a way to get clear on your personal brand.

What skills do you possess that you can speak honestly and confidently about?

_____

_____

_____

What do people say about you?

_____

_____

_____

What is your greatest strength?

_____

_____

_____

What type of information can you share to offer value?

_____

_____

_____

What are your passions?

_____

_____

_____

What type of personality do you have?

_____

_____

_____

What are your natural or learned gifts?

_____

_____

_____

What topics are you most often asked about?

_____

_____

_____

What problems are you solving with your book?

_____

_____

_____

What makes you stand out?

_____

_____

_____

How do you differ from others in your same niche?

_____

_____

_____

Here's a sample of my brand statement once I was done with this exercise:

> *I help authors and publishers promote their books online. I have 20 years of experience, which allows me to advise my clients and readers on the most effective and efficient methods for building their brand and promoting their books. I am enthusiastic and passionate about my work—some even call me a true believer. My curiosity and optimism has made me a natural risk-taker and has kept me ahead of the curve. My mission is to demystify online marketing and give practical, jargon-free advice.*

In this brand statement are clues about the content I share on social media. I usually give advice about book marketing, share my enthusiasm for all things digital, express the joy (and hardship) of being an entrepreneur, and keep my tone upbeat and optimistic. I may mention other things, but I quickly come back to the content that builds my brand.

Now it's your turn: Write down your brand message and look for clues for your brand voice.

_____

_____

_____

_____

_____

_____

_____

_____

One more exercise: Looking at my brand message, I could share information about:

1. _____

2. _____

3. _____

My brand voice is: _____ and _____

_____

Here are some examples of brand voice: *upbeat, optimistic, serious, creative, fun, hip, artsy, funny, silly, whimsical, personable, smart, educational, inspirational, helpful, trendy, classic, sassy*. Please stay away from *snarky*. It usually doesn't play well online.

Many people struggle with what to say and share on social media. These exercises should help you decide on your content and your voice. When in doubt, look at the list you've made and decide if the content you want to post fulfills your brand promise.

You've got a start on your personal brand. What should you think about next? Think big—explore your dreams for your book.

Chapter 2

You Gotta Dream Big

Without leaps of imagination, or dreaming, we
lose the excitement of possibilities. Dreaming,
after all, is a form of planning.
Gloria Steinem

Part of the reason I love my job is because I help authors make their dreams come true, but those dreams don't manifest instantly. Okay, they do for some—but those are the exceptions. To become a well-known and well-established professional author you have to be ready for the long haul, so adjust your expectations and remember that building an effective brand is a marathon, not a sprint.

This work is important, but it's not easy or quick. There may be an investment of years before you see the results you want. Or the results may look quite different from the ones you initially set out to achieve.

For now let's just explore this territory. The next step is to think of your dreams. Have fun with this list and check all that apply:

- ☐ I sell a zillion copies of my book.
- ☐ My business grows by 400 percent.
- ☐ I am on TV.
- ☐ I have my own TV show.
- ☐ I am on radio on big networks.
- ☐ I have a thoughtful interview on NPR.
- ☐ I have a special on PBS.
- ☐ I am on the cover of the *New York Times* book review section.
- ☐ I gain the respect of my peers in the academic world.
- ☐ My mom is really proud.
- ☐ *People* magazine features my book.
- ☐ The "real housewives" said my book saved their lives on a daytime talk show.
- ☐ My colleagues reviewed and praised my book.
- ☐ I speak at conferences, traveling 50 percent of my time.
- ☐ I am a regular contributor to Huffington Post and other popular online venues.
- ☐ I become rich from the sales of my book.
- ☐ I am on a reality TV show.
- ☐ I sell movie rights.
- ☐ I have 2,000 5-Star reviews on Amazon.

Keep going—these are *your* dreams after all …

_____

_____

_____

Keep this list of dreams handy because it will serve as an inspiration. As you begin the work of building a brand, there will be days when you may want to give up, days on which you feel no one out there is listening. But be patient. Slowly you will see signs of success—sometimes it just doesn't happen when you expect. It's like waiting for your baby's first smile. In fact, when I talk to my clients, I use a newborn as a metaphor for personal branding. I know it sounds crazy, but hear me out.

The first four weeks of parenting a newborn make for a one-way relationship. There is a whole lot of love flowing in your baby's direction, and a whole lot of work—feeding, changing, and soothing. Without a doubt, it's exhausting and at times frustrating. Day in and day out you adoringly devote yourself to your baby without any interaction back. But then, all of a sudden, your newborn looks into your eyes and smiles. Suddenly, your frustration melts away and you happily stay up all night and take care of your sweet baby.

That's what personal branding is like for me. In the beginning, it's all work. You wonder if anyone other than your mother is reading your blog. You feel a little defeated because you don't see immediate results from all of your outreach. "Where's the interaction or conversation?" you ask yourself. Rest assured, with patience and diligence your personal brand will become a relationship. If you attentively care for your baby—your personal brand—then your baby will smile back at you. You can't generate conversations overnight.

Care tenderly for your personal brand and you will reap the rewards of your efforts. One day everything will change for you. Someone will respond to you and let you know that your message matters. Someone will touch you by saying, "Thanks for what you wrote. It meant a lot to me." And that's the moment when you will stop asking, "Why am I doing this?"

Your day will come. Really. Trust me. As W. Clement Stone said, "Always aim for the Moon. Even if you miss, you'll land among the stars."

 Tip for #BusyAuthors

Remember to pace yourself and stay the course. It is easy to get discouraged if you don't see instant success.

Chapter 3

Know Thy Reader

The future of publishing is about having connections to readers and the knowledge of what those readers want.
Seth Godin

You now understand the value of building a brand and you've captured your dreams for your book. The next step is to figure out your audience, because you need to know how to find them and reach them. You need to know where your readers spend their time and what social media sites they visit. There's no point in learning to be the next Twitter expert if your audience is not even on Twitter.

Do you know where to find your readers based on what you know about them? Your answer is probably, "Kinda." Even if you think you know your readers, your ideas are probably way too broad. Over the years, authors have told me interesting things when it comes to their audience. Most of the time it's half the planet. "My audience is women," they tell me, or "it's people who have a job," or "people who have families." Being broad and general is not helpful when you are planning online marketing.

Understanding your readers is crucial because it will help you devise the best online strategy for you and your book. Online marketing is customized and personalized. It is essential for you to know your audience so you can serve them best. You should know their age group, gender, interests, and which social media outlets they use and where they hang out online. The more you know about them, the better your marketing will be.

Once I was working with a client who hired us to help brand her before her book came out. She is a nutritionist and works with children and their eating habits. You may think that is a narrow audience, but as we did the work we realized we needed to narrow the focus even more. Once we realized her message was resonating most with parents of toddlers, her campaign and messaging became much more focused and successful.

Remember, not all marketing ideas are good. An author once told me that he wanted to tell people about his book from the rooftop of the Apple Store in Manhattan using a megaphone. That might be a creative approach, but it probably would not have sold many books. Another author wanted to hire "hot girls" to hand out flyers on New York's Park Avenue. Again, the chances that a passerby will be a potential reader are low. If he wrote a graphic novel and wanted to pass out flyers at Comic-Con, that would be a different story. Always keep in mind your readers and where you can find them.

Questionnaire: Identifying your audience

Think about your readers. *Who are they?* Your inclination may be to answer, "Everyone"—but remember, there is no *everyone.com.* Just think about yourself as an audience for a minute. Do you read every type of book? Do all the magazine categories on newsstands appeal to you? Probably not.

We can all be identified (at least somewhat) by our interests. The more specific you can be in answering the reader profile questions below, the more successful your digital plan will be because it will be tailored to the needs of your specific audience. Take some time to consider your answers.

Base your answers on the majority of your readers. Of course, there will always be exceptions, but keep in mind that we are trying to build a plan for the majority. It is important to ask yourself the right questions and create a mental picture.

What about your readers? Let's try to figure them out

My Reader Profile
My reader is: Male or female or both_____.
Is _____ years old. (*Estimate a range. Just make a guess if you need to.*)
Lives in _____ (*setting or state or region, if relevant*)
Other books/authors/magazines/blogs he/she reads, and TV shows they watch:

_____

_____

_____

_____

_____

_____

What are some of the common values or traits of your ideal reader?

_____

_____

_____

_____

Does your audience have a problem, concern, or frustration that your book seeks to solve?

_____

_____

_____

What does your audience want?

_____

_____

_____

_____

What are the top three communities (health, business, fiction, romance ...) for the book?

_____

_____

_____

_____

What do you consider the top competitive titles for your book?

_____

_____

_____

_____

_____

_____

Education level of your readers:

_____

_____

Do they need/want your book for pleasure or business?

_____

_____

Is your reader on social networks?   Yes   No
Which ones?

_____

Notes: (*What else might you know about your reader? Go with your gut!*)

_____

_____

_____

_____

Here's what my reader profile looked like after I did this work:

> *My readers are authors or aspiring authors who are proactive about promoting their books. They are curious about online possibilities. My reader demographic is most likely an equal number of men and women, and*

in the age range of 35 and older and probably college educated. My readers have dabbled in social media like Facebook, Twitter, and LinkedIn. They are fulfilling a lifelong dream to tell their stories or to help others by sharing their knowledge. They are awesome—and they are very busy!

Your Reader Profile Statement (*compile all you have learned about your audience here*):

_____

_____

_____

_____

_____

_____

_____

_____

The value of knowing your readers

The identification of your ideal readers will play a major role in the quality of your online marketing plan. When I compare my reader profile against the demographics of different social networks, I can see clearly which networks will be helpful in my marketing. For example, my audience is going to be older than eighteen to twenty-nine, which accounts for the majority of the people on Instagram. So I can certainly join and have fun on Instagram, but it won't lead me to my readers. Since we are all busy, we have to make choices about how best to use our time, and knowing our audience will help us make better decisions.

Listing the demographics of all the social networks will get dated quickly, so if you are curious do a search for the information. I use Pew Research to get reliable data.

Before you move on to the next chapter, make sure you have a solid profile of your ideal reader. Identifying the community you want to create may take more time and energy up front, but it will save you time down the road.

 Tip for #BusyAuthors

Another benefit of filling out your reader profile: Once you have identified your readership base, you will know how to appeal to them and how to serve their needs. Your ideal community is more likely to provide you with reviews and become loyal to your brand.

Chapter 4

Get Real With Your Goals

People with clear, written goals accomplish far more in a shorter period of time than people without them could ever imagine.
Brian Tracy

There is an old joke that's been circling around the book publishing world since the 1930s.

Q: How do you make a small fortune in book publishing?
A: You start with a large one.

Book publishing is a labor of love for everyone. Yes, some authors make it big and get rich, but the rest of us work in book publishing because we love the written word. For every one of my clients publishing a book is a dream come true. Readers buying your book and absorbing your words is really a magical thing. To make your dreams a reality, we need to work on a plan.

You've spent time learning about online branding and why it is important. You have captured your dreams and refined your understanding of your readers. Now it's time to take all that thinking and turn it into concrete, clear goals that can make your dreams into a reality.

Let's start by asking an important question: What goals do you hope to achieve with your book? You want to be clear on your goals because why you sat down to write your book will shape how you promote your book and who you target.

▶ **Tip for #BusyAuthors**

It's important to write down your goals and the reasons for building a brand and post them where you can see them for inspiration. Building your brand and finding your audience is time consuming and can be challenging. You'll need inspiration when it gets difficult.

Begin by clarifying the answers to the following two questions:

Why did you write your book? (Your thinking on dreams should apply here.)

_____

_____

_____

_____

_____

Who is the audience for your book? (Your work on understanding your reader and capturing your reader profile applies here.)

_____

_____

_____

_____

As you answer these questions, a picture of your audience will emerge.

Nonfiction authors' goals are quite different from those of novelists. Nonfiction authors may want to shed light on an untold story, share their knowledge, teach, build a platform, showcase an expertise, build a business, acquire clients, and get speaking engagements. Novelists, on the other hand, usually want to tell a story that must be told. Novelists often want to share a story that has lived in their minds for years and that they must get on the page.

Whether you are an author of fiction or nonfiction, you most likely share a common motivation—wanting people to buy and love your books.

To move your big-picture dreams closer to earth, think about the following statements and check all that apply to your goals:

☐ I want a three-book deal with a large advance from a publisher so I can just write full time.

☐ I want to bring a story to light and expose a truth.

☐ I want to share my knowledge and expertise.

☐ I want my book to help grow my business.

☐ I want to become a speaker or launch workshops in my area of expertise.

☐ I want to position myself as an expert in a particular niche.

- ☐ I want my own radio/TV show.
- ☐ I want people to benefit from my work.
- ☐ I want to tell an entertaining story.
- ☐ I want to be the next great American novelist.

Keep going. These are your goals. No one has to see this list, but the act of making it will help you plan your priorities.

_____

_____

_____

_____

▶ **Tip for #BusyAuthors**

It's really important to know that wanting a bestselling book is a wish and not a goal. Goals should be SMART (Specific, Measurable, Attainable, Realistic, Timely). Writing a book is a goal that can be achieved by setting a specific timeline and writing regularly, but writing a bestseller can't be divided into tasks. If we knew how to make a bestseller, everyone in publishing would do it over and over again.

Your next step is to drill down to your value proposition by asking yourself these questions and writing out your answers:

1. How does your book benefit others?

_____

_____

_____

_____

2. How is your book different from others?

_____

_____

_____

3. Who does it help?

_____

_____

_____

_____

4. Does your book solve a problem and offer a solution? Explain.

_____

_____

_____

_____

Once you have spent time on this exercise, write down your specific goals. Get your goal statement in writing so you can read it regularly and remember why (your motivation) you are doing the extra work it will take to promote your book and build your brand. After I did this work, my goal statement looked something like this:

> *I want to write a book so I can help authors who want to be proactive about promoting their books. I have spent my entire career helping authors one-on-one, and that model is not scalable. I want to share my knowledge and expertise with authors and aspiring authors. If I make any money it would be used for travel with my family (maybe we'd go to Bali, which is on our bucket*

list). If I sell a few copies, we'll go for a nice dinner. Overall, I want to help authors realize their online marketing potential.

Now it's your turn.

The goals for writing my book:

_____

_____

_____

_____

_____

_____

_____

Remember, your goals will help you decide on the types of things you do and how much time you spend doing them. Your goals determine where you are headed, what you hope to achieve with your book promotion, and how to craft your message.

Time to dig deeper for secondary goals

Selling books is almost always the first goal of every author. However, if you chat with authors a bit they'll say things like ...

I want to help people.
I want to help business people learn new skills and strategies.
I want small businesses to succeed.
I want to share my experience with a startup.
I know my book will make a difference.
I want to make sure people know the truth about what's really going on.

I want to make people laugh.

I want to entertain my readers.

I envision a world where people love what they do, and if they read my book they would.

Add your own ...

I often take on projects based on these secondary goals, the goals that speak to the deeper truth of the person and the importance of the book. These are the goals that are worth talking about.

As a marketer, I can tell you that no conversation has ever started from "please buy my book because I would like to have a bestseller." It's those secondary goals that get people talking. Authenticity and vulnerability connect and resonate online and offline.

As of today, plug into those secondary goals so you can get on with the business of starting conversations.

My secondary goals are:

_____

_____

_____

_____

_____

_____

_____

Marketing is truly about conversations and social media. So if you are going to spend the time and money marketing your book, you should always ask yourself:

- Will my actions start, maintain, or enhance the conversation?
- Will this get people talking?
- Will they share, post, or retweet this?

In my experience, a sustained effort to keep people talking results in speaking engagements, paid blog posts (yes, there is such a thing), interview opportunities, more fans on your Facebook page, more traffic on your site, increased sales, and a recognition and expansion of your online brand.

 Tip for #BusyAuthors

The age of generalists is over. Find a niche, develop your audience, hone your skills, and be brilliant.

Chapter 5

Best Advice in the Business

Our goals can only be reached through a vehicle
of a plan, in which we must fervently believe,
and upon which we must vigorously act.
There is no other route to success.
Pablo Picasso

In the first few chapters, we spent time getting to know your dreams and goals. To make them a reality, we now need a solid plan and some good advice from people who do this work well.

To help you craft the right online marketing mix and to ensure that the conversations you start with your readers are effective, I tapped into the collective intelligence of book publishing professionals and asked: What is the one marketing tip you would give to authors? Here is what they said:

Advice from publishers and agents

Know your readers: "Nothing works all the time, or for everyone. It's important for authors to leave no stone unturned and consider how social media can work for them, but also important to consider the whole picture of getting the word out about their book and reaching readers. I'm sure there are examples of authors whose success is directly related to their social media strategy and efforts. But there also are authors whose success has come mostly without that. Without diving too deeply into it, I think there are different kinds of readers who use and don't use social media in different ways. When there's a match between an author's efforts and the potential readers they are reaching, that can be magic. But when there isn't, a lot of energy can go to waste. Things are always changing in the social media world. The best advice I can give is to write the best book you can and reassess your social media involvement/strategy often."

Stephanie Rostan, principal at
Levine Greenberg Rostan Literary

Develop a long-term relationship with your readers: "Engaging with readers on Facebook is a lot of work and the reward for doing so may not be apparent during the publication of your first book, but it could develop into a great platform to help with the launch of your second."

Peter Costanzo, digital publishing
specialist at the Associated Press

Be real: "Be authentic in your Facebook and Twitter postings. When you post about things you care about, aside from your book, you develop a closer connection to your followers. They'll pay more attention when you do post about your book because they won't feel like you're only just trying to sell it to them. And they'll be more likely to share or retweet your posts to their friends because you've established a common ground."

Patty Berg, director of retail
marketing, Crown Publishing Group

Trust your publisher: "I think the one piece of advice I'd give authors is that 9.9 times out of 10 they should trust their publishers. Publishers want to sell copies as much as anybody. Collaborating with them with a smile will get you everywhere!"

Kate Lloyd, associate director of publicity
at Scribner/Simon & Schuster

Build a community: "Books don't create movements, movements create books." We at Berrett-Koehler think this is a succinct way of capturing the idea that you can't expect a book to create a community to support your book. You have to build a community of fans and advocates around your ideas and then the right book to write and publish will be born out of the need to publish that content in book form to further your movement and ideas."

Kristen Frantz, vice president of sales and
marketing, Berrett-Koehler Publishers

Enjoy yourself: "One marketing tip I would give to authors is to stick with a social platform you *enjoy*. You may be able to write 140-character ideas at a fast clip, but your creativity won't benefit your cause (in this case, your *book*) unless it feels genuine. Besides, you have enough on your plate. Why not love your marketing process as well?"

Kate Rados, director, community development, Crown Publishing

Take the lead: "The best marketing advice I can give to authors is to do everything you can to take the lead on marketing yourself and your book. While the publisher is your partner in this, it is ultimately up to *you* to maximize your opportunities and do everything possible leading up to and after your book's publication."

Wendy Sherman, literary agent and founder of Wendy Sherman Associates

 Tip for #BusyAuthors

Go digital. Start early. Be authentic.

Advice from authors

Plan for the long game: "The real quick learning for me is: to focus more on the long game instead of anchoring all your hopes and expectations around the launch week. I have learned that the bigger goal over time is to build your book's content into almost everything you do over the following years. Then another important element is trying to build a backlist of multiple books that continue to have influence over the span of decades."

Tom Rath, author of six influential bestsellers, including *Are You Fully Charged?* and *StrengthsFinder 2.0*

Start early: "Start building your social media platform well in advance of launching your book. If authors are not prepared to do a lot of digital marketing and most of it on their own dime they might as well not write the book unless purely for vanity."

August Turak, author of *Business Secrets of the Trappist Monks: One CEO's Quest for Meaning and Authenticity*

Keep your name out there: "I'd suggest keeping in contact with your readers—either through Facebook, Twitter, or old-fashioned email—and writing as many articles as you can to keep your name out there and to get to know different bloggers."

Adam Mitzner, author of *Losing Faith, A Case of Redemption*, and *A Conflict of Interest*

Get help: "My advice is to prep early and often—make sure you have a professional author site, a Facebook author page, and a tweeting presence (though I'm not at all convinced that tweeting helps to sell any books!). And though your publisher will assign a digital and a conventional publicist to you, you won't get the attention you need to get your book really out there. The in-house publicists are already overworked.

"You'll need to hire an outside publicist and the question is: conventional, digital, or both? The choice will be yours, so ask other authors whom they use and be sure to ask for the details. Was the campaign a success? What's the cost? What's your involvement? If you can only use one, digital marketing, which is so foreign to most of us, is likely your best bet. In this digital age, we need all the help we can get. Don't be afraid to ask for it."

Roberta Gately, author of *The Bracelet*
and *Lipstick in Afghanistan*

Spend to market: "Authors should understand that no matter how much support they get from their publishers, they will need to think of becoming authors as launching a business. They are now CEOs of ongoing enterprises that will demand great marketing, great PR, and new products. So they should be prepared to settle in for the long haul in this new role."

Jan Ellison, author of *A Small Indiscretion*

► **Tip for #BusyAuthors**

You don't have to be an early adopter and chase every new social media tool. Use tools that have a track record for success.

Chapter 6

Your Priority List

Only by carving out think-time and reflection can
we actually understand, in an entirely different
context, the actions we take.
Daniel Patrick Forrester

Most authors think of online marketing as a directive to "go start tweeting" or "go start blogging." But as you can see from the work you have already done in the first few chapters, just tweeting without understanding why is not only frustrating, it's also ineffective and unsustainable. Before you can dive in, you need to consider your priorities.

As you know by now, I believe in the value of developing an online brand, but it does not rule my life. I try to be strategic in my use of time and effort. Like you, I have other, more important priorities. So let's just try to keep all of this in perspective. If you start to feel overwhelmed, take a break and reread your lists of goals and dreams for some encouragement.

Tip for #BusyAuthors

When you look at all the different elements of online marketing, you may feel overwhelmed. But here's the thing: You don't have to do it all. You can start slow and small and grow gradually.

Here's your priority list

By now you have thought long and hard about your goals and priorities, you've read advice from publishing experts, and I hope you are convinced that online marketing is a must-do activity for you.

It's time to make a priority list. To successfully market your book, you'll need to develop a plan that works best for your readers. Digital branding works only when it is customized for you and your readers. There is no one-size-fits-all method.

Follow the steps below to develop a priority list. While you might be tempted to skip a few steps, don't give in to that temptation. Each step can make the crucial difference between the success and failure of your online marketing.

There are six essential elements (and two others that are nice to have) for successful online branding. When used together, they make for a powerful combination. Once you have mastered these elements, you can add other options, but first make sure your foundation is solid. More details on each will follow in the upcoming chapters.

1. Website. A professional website is the single most important step toward your digital branding. Your website is your home base, so make sure it is updated regularly and is current.

Use your site as a platform for all other activities. Post your blogs and photos along with links to your social networks. Always remember your audience when developing content. If a person cares enough to come to your site, you need to make sure their trip was worth the effort. Remember: It doesn't have to be fancy or expensive to look professional.

2. Mailing List. Email is still the most powerful digital tool. You may hear people say that email is so yesterday. Don't believe them. For many of my clients, the open rate for their newsletters is over 50 percent. No other activity will give you that kind of return. Every single author should have a mailing list. You should encourage readers to sign up for your mailing list. Over time the email addresses of your readers will become one of your biggest and most valuable assets. You can communicate with your readers through a regular email newsletter sent either once a month or once every three months. Just keep those lines of communication open. Value your subscribers, since they are your biggest fans and advocates. Remember that you must have their permission to talk with them. Don't send a mass email message without their permission, because you will leave a bad taste in their mouth. You will be telling them that they will get your message whether they want it or not. Now what would that say about your brand?

There are also legal implications of sending emails without permission. More on that in a later chapter.

3. Blog. A blog is the best way to share your expertise and drive traffic to your site. Use your blog on your own website along with posting it on an important high-traffic website as a guest post. Everyone needs content, and it never hurts to ask a popular blog if they want to run your blog post. Blogs don't have to be long: blogs of 700 to 1,000 words are typically most effective. Google has recently started rewarding sites with longer blogs with better search results. Long-form content (2,000 words or more) increases page authority, and Google weighs them more when providing search results. This is good news for many of my clients who like to write longer blogs.

4. LinkedIn. A LinkedIn profile is a must-have for all of us. Even if you are not very active on it, it is a good idea to fill out the profile in as much detail as possible. Most people who may want to do business with you will certainly review your LinkedIn profile. It's a great way to break the ice and get to know someone quickly. You should start building your network long before you need it.

5. Facebook. I know Facebook is no longer the coolest network, but for most of my clients it is the most effective. Facebook is an important element of digital branding and, with more than 1 billion people on it, you can't afford to ignore it. You may be wondering if you need both a personal profile page and an author fan page. My advice is yes—these profiles serve different audiences and purposes. In your profile page, you can engage with family and friends and readers. Most of my clients find the most support on their Facebook page. They can get 300 Likes on their author photo, for example. This is your personal network, and these people will help you in ways no one else will. So hold on to your personal profile and stay connected with your network.

Facebook pages have other benefits. Facebook has changed the algorithm so your fan page gets less traffic without spending money to boost your post. It is also true that many of your connections may never migrate to the "author" page, so you may wonder what the point is. One key benefit of having a page is that you can use the data provided in Insights and do geographically targeted advertising. This type of advertising is really helpful when you want people who are interested in your topic to come to your event. For example, you can target people who live five to twenty miles from the event location. We have used this type of advertising for many of our clients, and every time we have seen bigger turnouts than expected.

According to Facebook, "Personal profiles are for non-commercial use and represent individual people. You can follow profiles to see public updates from people you're interested in but aren't friends with. Pages look similar to personal profiles, but they offer unique tools for businesses, brands, and organizations. Pages are managed by people who have personal profiles. You can like a Page to see updates in News Feed. Keep in mind that each person who signs up for Facebook has one account with login information. Each account can have one personal profile and manage multiple Pages."

6. Twitter. I know many authors are intimidated by Twitter, but it's a fabulous way to share resources and develop a following. I think Twitter is an incredible tool for listening and for doing market research. You can listen to your readers, find out what other people are doing and saying, and build a relationship with current and future readers.

7. Goodreads. Some authors love Goodreads and the community they have built there. These authors have successful giveaways, which makes their books popular on Goodreads. I suggest that you set up a profile, plan or ask your publisher to do a galley giveaway, and participate if you are making good connections. Once a week you can check in, rate books, add books to your bookshelf and check out interesting discussions.

8. Video. If you are like me, you may not be very comfortable with seeing yourself on video. However, there is no better or easier way to show your passion and personality than on video. It can be fun or useful content for your Facebook fan page, your blog, and/or your website. So if you can get over the hesitation, it would be worth trying.

▶ **Tip for #BusyAuthors**

Talking to people is a privilege: Don't waste it. It is much better to have a small mailing list of interested people than a large one filled with people who aren't interested.

Your personal interests and skills will determine what you do and how much time you spend on each element. For example, like many of my clients you may like to write blogs because they give you a natural avenue to express yourself. Most of my authors start off liking (and being comfortable with) one social media channel rather than another. For now, just think about where you'd like to put your time and effort. You can always change your mind or add other elements as you get more comfortable. Tomorrow there may be a shiny new digital tool that you may want to add to the mix. Just don't lose track of the essentials.

 Tip for #BusyAuthors

When your book is listed on Amazon, fill out the author profile in as much detail as possible.

Phase 2
Turning Your Thinking Into Action

Chapter 7

Your Online Marketing Plan

You have brains in your head.
You have feet in your shoes.
You can steer yourself in any
Direction you choose.
You're on your own.
And you know what you know.
And YOU are the one who'll decide where to go ...
Dr. Seuss

In my experience, making a tangible plan allows you to start strong and maintain your enthusiasm for the extra work of marketing both your book and yourself. In this chapter we'll assess where you are and what you'll need to make a successful plan.

You'll have to make some important decisions to make sure your plan is sustainable and scalable. Here's another exercise to help you move forward with a plan.

Assess your current situation

Maybe you are just starting out and you don't have a website up yet. Or maybe you have a website and a few social media platforms in place, but you haven't devoted time to managing your social media pages yet. Take some time to assess your situation. This first step is perhaps the most important. Before you can commit to doing more digital branding, you need to assess where you are today and know what's working and what's not. Take a snapshot of where you stand by asking yourself the following questions. If the answer is no or if you know you need to do more work in the area, add it to your to-do list provided at the end of the chapter.

It's okay to start from scratch—or to ramp up what you've already got in place. There are no wrong answers here; it's just an exercise to gauge where you are in the process and determine what steps to take next.

 Tip for #BusyAuthors

Answering these questions will help you identify your current online marketing status and decide where to focus and begin.

Website
Do you have a website?　☐ Yes　☐ No

If you don't have a website, skip the next few questions. And add getting a website to your to-do list.

How well is your website working for your goals?

_____

_____

_____

_____

_____

_____

If you pay attention to traffic on your site, write down your answers to the best of your knowledge. If not, we will cover it in the website chapter.

How many people come to your site? _____

Which pages do they visit? _____

How do they find you?: _____

How long do they stay? _____

If people aren't staying on your website for more than a few seconds, then something needs to change.

Mailing list

Do you have email addresses of your readers?   ☐ Yes ☐ No

Do you have a method for collecting emails in one place? ☐ Yes ☐ No

(*MailChimp or Constant Contact are popular list hosting sites.*)

Having a mailing list is an important part of your strategy, so if you are not actively collecting and using names, add that to your to-do list.

If you have a list, how often do you communicate with them?

_____

_____

If your schedule is less than ideal, add "communicate more often with subscribers" to your to-do list.

Blog

Blogging is the foundation for content on your website, so it is important to figure out a schedule and a content strategy. We'll talk more about that later, but for now just put down where you stand today.

Are you currently writing a blog?   ☐ Yes   ☐ No

_____

_____

_____

_____

Which blog topics are most popular?

_____

_____

_____

_____

What are the three topics you want to write about?

_____

_____

_____

_____

Social Media

Social Network	Yes or No	Number of Fans/ Followers
LinkedIn		
Facebook		
Twitter		
Goodreads		
Instagram		
Pinterest		
Tumblr		
YouTube		
Snapchat		

Are you directing followers to your website from social media? ☐ Yes ☐ No

_____

_____

_____

_____

Content

Do you have the resources in place to develop content and keep your online conversation going? The resources here can be time or help from a family member or an intern or an assistant.

_____

_____

_____

_____

How much time, knowledge, technology, or money do you have to devote to your digital branding effort?

_____

_____

_____

For your digital strategy to be effective, you also need to be a storyteller, marketer, and brand evangelist. It's important for you to decide how much time you can dedicate to crafting your story and message, writing blogs, and reaching out to your target audience. If you don't have the time (an hour or two a day) to devote to these efforts, you may need to figure out how to get some help. Make a plan to set aside several hours a week. I know: You're busy, but being organized will help you make the most out of that time.

How much time can you commit to your online marketing?

_____

_____

_____

Without setting realistic goals and timelines you will not know when you are making progress, achieving success, or missing the mark. Depending on your answers to these questions, some realistic goals could include some of the following possibilities.

Use this to-do list to get organized about the things you need to do next. Check all that apply to you:

Website
- ☐ Create a website.
- ☐ Improve your website.
- ☐ Figure out how much traffic you are attracting to your website.
- ☐ _____
- ☐ _____

Mailing list
- ☐ Build a mailing list.
- ☐ Sign up for email software.
- ☐ Add a way for people to sign up on your mailing list.
- ☐ Communicate more often with subscribers.
- ☐ _____
- ☐ _____

Blog
- ☐ Write blogs a couple of times a month or more.
- ☐ Decide on the content.
- ☐ Make a list of sites where you can guest blog (_hint: where your readers hang out_).
- ☐ _____
- ☐ _____

Social networking
- ☐ Figure out a content plan.
- ☐ Post daily or several times a week.
- ☐ Learn to design graphics and/or record video.
- ☐ Sign up for two or three social networks.
- ☐ Make sure the social network profiles are filled out as completely as possible.
- ☐ Reach out to your network and start linking with people.
- ☐ Start helping others.
- ☐ _____
- ☐ _____

Many of these tools may be new to you, and it can take a while to learn them. You may consider taking an online or offline class. We use lynda.com at our office for online video courses and to keep our skills current. Or you can get help from the library or a friend or family member. It's a good idea to make an ongoing investment in your online education and set aside a couple of hours a week (at least) to read blogs and take classes.

Online marketing changes all the time so it's important that you keep an open mind and experiment. If you succeed in creating engagement, learn from it and try it again. If you fail, just smile. Take a deep breath, and try something else.

The best part about online marketing is that it is an innovative field and you can try different things in different combinations. You just have to find the right combination for you and your readers. In the next chapters, we'll take each element of successful online branding and discuss it in more detail.

► Tip for #BusyAuthors

There is no one-size-fits-all marketing plan for every author. Each author needs a customized online marketing plan.

Chapter 8

Building Your Website

*My website is a terrific marketing tool and provides an
attractive, friendly forum for interacting with my readers.*
Sue Grafton, author of many #1
New York Times *bestsellers*

In 1996, we developed one of the first author websites. It was
for Sue Grafton. Not many companies get the privilege of
starting their web development business with a #1 *New York
Times* bestselling author. My husband and I worked for days
to get the background color and texture just right. It was a
thrilling time for us. Sue was delighted. The page on the site
that was the most popular was one about Sue's cats. Her fans
would come to her book signings and ask about her cats, and
Sue would direct her fans to the site where they could see the
cat photos. A website can connect you with your readers in a
personal way.

Why have a website?

In 1997, having an author website was such an unusual event that the *New York Times* covered it as a trend. Today, however, every author needs a professional website, and an author website is no longer news.

Websites are a crucial link between you and your readers. It is the one place, the hub, of all your activities. Your website is your opportunity to connect with your readers in a personal way. It is also where you have full control (unlike other social media sites) over your brand, so you will want to review your goals from earlier chapters and make sure your website addresses those goals and reflects your personal brand. A few questions to ask yourself:

- Does your website represent your brand visually through its design?
- Does your website reflect your secondary goals?
- Is your website designed for the audience you have identified?
- If your book was written to solve a problem or offer a solution, does your website do the same?

 Tip for #BusyAuthors

Make sure your website is tailored specifically to achieve your goals. A lot has changed in the last five years, and if you had a site that was developed before then, you may want to consider redesigning your site.

Building your website

If you are a little bit tech savvy, you can design a site yourself. WordPress can be an excellent platform for your website. Just make sure that the site looks professional and reflects well on your personal brand. WordPress is engineered to be user friendly, and it can be highly customized with plugins (packaged lines of code that quickly install into WordPress). Plus, the code in WordPress-hosted websites is designed for the best possible search engine optimization (SEO), ensuring that if people go looking for you on Google, they are likely to find your website.

There are a lot more website development tools available today, like wix.com and Squarespace. If you are curious, check them out. At this time, WordPress is the most popular website platform for a reason, and we use it to develop most of our websites.

My personal advice for you would be to hire a web designer. I am tech savvy, but I am not a designer. Sites designed by professional designers and developers look professional and are well organized. You want to be able to update the site yourself, but it is a good investment to hire a professional to design it.

When looking at a web design firm, ask your agent or fellow authors for their recommendations. It is best to use a design firm that specializes in author websites. If that's not their specialty, make sure that they have done a few author websites you like. The design is, of course, important—but just as important is the organization and architecture of the site, so make sure you review those aspects of sample websites as well.

One of my clients had his website designed by his daughter's friend. She was a good designer and had creative ideas. However, her priority was the look of the site and its cool factor for her portfolio. The site lacked basic information that an author website needs, like bibliographic details on the book and links to the publisher and to booksellers. There was no excerpt from the book or any way to sign up for a mailing list. If you are working with a new firm, make sure you are giving them detailed information both on the design and on the content and goals.

It's a good idea to ask for proposals from at least two or three companies so you can compare them, but remember to compare apples to apples. Some people charge per page to design and develop a site (which makes no sense to me), and others may charge a high hosting fee or may not be available to update your site after it has launched. Make sure you look at all the elements of the project, not just the price. Any good firm should be able to do basic search engine optimization work for you, but be sure to ask about it.

I know budget is always a consideration when we think about marketing, but a well-designed website will be worth the investment in the long run.

 Tip for #BusyAuthors

Keep in mind that we do judge a book by its cover and people will judge the quality of your work and writing by the professionalism of your website.

Your website checklist

☐ **Go mobile.**

We are dealing with a social and mobile reader, so make sure that the design of your website is mobile-friendly. Google will penalize your mobile search results if you do not have a responsive design. It's important to make navigation easy. Consider that people may be using fingers rather than their mouse to move around. Large graphics and dark colors are not ideal for reading on mobile devices.

☐ **It's all in the name.**

Your website should be under your name, and it should be about you and your brand and not just your book. Readers follow and identify with people/authors and not books alone. Even if you publish multiple books with multiple publishers, all of which have their own websites, you need a site in your name as an author. You can link to all the other sites, or, better yet, bring all the information under one umbrella site. You can always have other URLs redirected to your new site.

☐ **Generate visual interest.**

Use good design and relevant graphics to represent your brand, but don't just grab them from the web. Respect other people's work and the copyright laws. You can buy stock photos or take your own photos. (I'll say more about photos and images later on.)

☐ **Write your bio.**

Have a great bio page. Let your readers get to know you. List your background and accomplishments, career highlights, and how you became passionate about your particular area of expertise. Feature your photos and other images. This is your opportunity to connect with your readers. Put some personality into your bio page.

☐ **Create a book page.**

Write up a promotional preview of your book. Consider adding more information, like your motivations for writing the book. Maybe a short, creative video about your book would be fun.

☐ **Make buying easy.**

Wherever you mention your book, make sure you have links to booksellers. It's important to link to Amazon, B&N, Books-a-Million, IndieBound, iBooks, and your publisher (if you have one). Instead of adding links to their homepages, link directly to your book page on their website. Make buying as easy as possible.

☐ **Have a newsletter signup.**

One of the main benefits of having a website is that it gives you a place to collect names and emails and build your following. Connect to your readers on a consistent basis with an email newsletter. Your subscribers are your Super Fans (more on this in the next chapter). You can use your newsletter to discuss various topics in your industry, promote your book or blog, and offer favorite snippets from your book. You have lots of choices.

☐ **Have a contact page visible on your homepage.**

Don't make people search your website to find you. Have a Contact button on your homepage. You can decide what contact information you'd like to make public, but provide a way for people to contact you with ease. If you want to build your following, you want people to be able to easily connect with you and ask questions. And unless you have a compelling reason not to, make sure you write back.

☐ **Display your testimonials.**
Your testimonial page can be as simple as a list of quotes from readers and other experts in your field touting your expertise or raving about your book. Short quotes are more compelling than long letters or references on your website, so opt for brief and impactful.

☐ **Create a tour/speaking page, if applicable.**
If you want to speak or if you go on a book tour, list the events on your speaking page. List the places where you have made speaking appearances and provide a summary of the topics you speak most often about.

☐ **Highlight press coverage.**
Anytime you receive press coverage—whether print, TV, radio, or online—link it to your site. Not only does featuring media coverage increase your name and brand credibility, but it typically leads to more media opportunities.

☐ **Link up socially.**
It's important to have links to your social networks (which should also be in your name) and ways to share your site on social networks. Add the social share buttons for any of your networks: Facebook, Twitter, YouTube, Pinterest, LinkedIn, Tumblr, Instagram, etc.

☐ **Blog because content is king.**
Many of my clients hate to blog. Who has the time? Yet the benefits of blogging are numerous. Blogs help you establish your brand, bring traffic to your site from searches, and showcase your expertise.

☐ **Monitor your site.**

Once you have the basics of your website up and running, it's important to gauge how your website is doing. You don't have to become a web wizard, but having a working knowledge of your website analytics is helpful in maintaining an effective website. When you build a site to meet certain goals—as everyone should—you need to be able to assess whether you are meeting those goals. You should always know how people are getting to your site so you can increase your traffic.

▶ **Tip for #BusyAuthors**

Starting early (months or years before the publication of your book) gives you time to make mistakes, learn from them, and make improvements.

Google Analytics

If you have a website, you need to know if it's working for you. It's important to find out what specifically is working well so you can do more of it. It's great if your mom is visiting your website, but not so great if *only* your mom is visiting your website. The easiest and most effective way to track your website progress and discover what's resonating with your visitors is connecting your site to Google Analytics with a little bit of tracking code. Let's take a look at some of the benefits of tracking your site's traffic with Google Analytics.

**If you can't measure it, you can't manage it.
Or, what isn't tracked can't be improved.**

It's easy to use Google Analytics to analyze the traffic data for your website. The software is free, and your website developer should be able to add the tracking code.

Google Analytics can tell you a lot of crucial information about your website at a glance. If you are new to it, you can check out their website for lots of free information. If you are already familiar with tracking website analytics, here's the data you should collect and review:

Number of visits. Your number of visits is the number of times someone comes to your site. If the same person comes back more than once, that's tracked as two visits.

Unique visitors. The number of new people coming to your site. Each unique person is counted once.

Page views. Page views are the number of pages on your site that were viewed. Each link on a website takes you to a new page. An increase in page views indicates that more content is being viewed across your website. You can see where people are going on your site and how many pages they view per visit.

Bounce rate. The bounce rate is the percentage of people who see one page and then leave the site or "bounce" off the page. Aim for a low bounce rate (under 20 percent). Low rates mean that people are finding content they like and that you are likely achieving reader engagement.

Average time on the site. This metric indicates how long someone stays on your site. This is a good number to track to see if it's improving or declining. The more content you have, the longer people will stay.

Top content. Track the content that gets the most page views and the highest traffic to show your best-performing pages. That will tell you what works so that you can do more of it.

Referrals. It's really important to see where your traffic is coming from. If you blog for a news site or a third-party site and they are sending no traffic to your site, then it's probably not a mutually beneficial relationship. However, if a site is sending you lots of qualified traffic (meaning that when people come they tend to stay), then it would be valuable to increase your engagement with that referral site.

Social visits. Find out what social media sites send the most traffic to your website by going to the Traffic Sources section of Google Analytics and click "All Traffic." You will be able to see the websites and social networks that send traffic to your site.

Traffic source keywords. Track the keywords people use on search engines to get to your site. Find out which keywords are associated with a low bounce rate, high time on site, and lots of page visits—they are the ones you should use in your blog post titles and as tags and categories. Your keywords also can be a good indication of the content that resonates with your readers.

SEO

Keyword search engine optimization is important because it
helps search engines find your site easily. Manipulating SEO
results may not always be effective. I have seen sites that are so
loaded with keywords that it's difficult to read them. I believe
you should design your site for humans, not for search engines. People expect authentic communication, not marketing
copy. Make sure that your site isn't so optimized for SEO that
it doesn't read well.

If you are considering hiring an SEO firm, make sure you
understand your goals. Most good SEO companies will increase traffic to your site, but it may not always be good, or
what I call qualified, traffic. It may bring traffic by "tricking"
search engines with keywords, but once people get to your site
they may leave because they are not finding what they expected. I knew one author (a New York doctor) who spent $10,000
a month with an SEO firm (I kid you not). He told me that
his traffic had increased tenfold but that it was not bringing
in new patients to his practice. I asked him to forward the
traffic reports to me. On closer inspection I realized he was
only seeing the increase in the number of visitors, which was
impressive. But I wanted to dig deeper, so I asked for the full

traffic report. Within minutes I could see that the strategic keywords were bringing people to his sites, but the visitors were not looking for a doctor so within a few seconds they bounced off. His bounce rate was 88 percent, and his average time-on-site was ten seconds. No wonder all that extra traffic was not producing new patients. It's better to attract the right people than to attract a lot of people.

Chapter 9

Mailing List of Fans

Coming together is a beginning; keeping together is progress; working together is success.
Henry Ford

People on your mailing list are your Super Fans. They are the people who have given you permission to show up in their inbox, and that invitation is of great value to you. Think about it: When was the last time you signed up for a newsletter? Most likely you are selective in what emails you want to see in your inbox. Once I asked an author that question and she said, "Oh, I don't do that." She's right. We don't do that unless we are Super Fans, or unless the author is providing us with something of value.

Why have a mailing list?
Social media is sexy, but the real power of your relationship with your fans is in your mailing list. You own your mailing

list and have access to it anytime you need it. More than once, I have seen authors lose all their followers on Twitter because of a glitch in the system. Besides, not everyone is on social media, but almost everyone has an email address. The cost is low and the returns are high. Don't let people tell you email is so yesterday. Email newsletters for authors have more engagement than social media.

Your email subscribers are often the first in line to buy your books, show up at your events, and recommend you to others. With the slightest encouragement, Super Fans engage with you on social media. Your most important marketing task is to keep your Super Fans happy and engaged.

A word of caution: The CAN-SPAM Act was put in place in 2003. It has clear guidelines for what is and is not legal. Here are a few to keep in mind:

- There are rules about buying, selling, and renting email lists. Overall, it's a good idea not to do any of that.
- The subject line should not be deceptive.
- There has to be an unsubscribe option.
- Your mailing list should be made up of people who signed up for your mailing list (for example, you can't add someone's email address to your mailing list just because you are connected with them on LinkedIn or you exchanged emails with them last year).

Obviously, I am not a lawyer, so please review the law for yourself. For me, the bottom line is that you need to respect your readers and treat them as you would want to be treated. No one wants spam. All you need to do is to take the extra step of getting permission.

Checklist for your mailing list

☐ **Grow your list.**

Make sure it is easy to sign up for your mailing list. Have a link on your website and your social networks where people can sign up to be on your email list. Consider offering something for free when people sign up. Some ideas include a tips list, cheat sheet, video interview, or anything else that offers value to your reader. Just make sure to keep the offerings in sync with your brand.

☐ **Be consistent.**

It's not always easy, but try to keep a schedule. Share useful information, resources, and special offers throughout the year. Talking to people on your mailing list is a privilege. Don't just email them when you have something to sell.

☐ **Don't overdo it.**

Likewise, it's best not to send mailings too often. (Retailers learned how quickly we unsubscribed when they sent too many offers.) You should know your Super Fans best, so plan accordingly. Once a month is probably right. Once every three months is most common. Just don't do it only to promote a new book. You should communicate with your fans even when you have nothing to promote.

☐ **Use software.**

There are excellent email newsletter solutions out there. The most popular are Constant Contact, and MailChimp. I've used both and think that Constant Contact is easier to use, but MailChimp is more cost-effective. So do a little research and find the best fit for your needs. These recommendations can get dated over time. If a new, better software hits the market I will update it on my website: www.fauziaburke.com. Please join Book Updates at www.fauziaburke.com/bookupdates and I'll send you an alert every time I add new information.

☐ **Design it.**
People don't read email newsletters, they scan them. So make sure that your email design is easy to scan with images and links for more information. Most people won't read a block of text that is 1,000 words long. Keep the design consistent with your website and use images to capture their attention.

☐ **Customize your content.**
The purpose of your newsletter is to develop and further enrich your relationship with your Super Fans. So add a personal note and make sure the copy does not sound like an infomercial. Keep it short and add links for more information. Entertain, educate, solve a problem, and offer value.

☐ **Be personal.**
Be personal and friendly. Write emails that are conversational.

☐ **Track results.**
The best part about using mail software is that it gives you lots of analytics and other feedback information. You can find out not only who is on your list and whether your list is growing or shrinking but also what content and headlines work best for your list. Every time you do a mailing, you should assess the results a week later. Try out different subject lines to see which ones work best.

☐ **Adjust your timing.**

There is a good time to send out a newsletter. GetResponse analyzed 2.1 million messages and discovered that the top engagement times are between 8 a.m. and 10 a.m. and 3 p.m. to 4 p.m. EST. The best day to send out a newsletter is midweek. Using these windows of time can increase the open rate of your emails. However, it is important to know your own readers. For example, I get the highest open rate when I send my newsletter out at 3 p.m. on a Friday. So experiment a bit before you settle on a time and day that works best for your readers.

☐ **Create special offers.**

As Super Fans, your mailing list subscribers have earned the right to a few perks. So if you want someone to get an early peek at your book or vote on the jacket design, this is the group to work with. Consider hosting a Super Fan–only event or other fun events. Get creative! You may discover other cool ways to stay connected and engaged with your mailing list subscribers.

Your Super Fans are among your biggest assets. Take great care to cultivate your relationship with them and stay engaged and connected.

▶ **Tip for #BusyAuthors**

People who sign up to your mailing list are your Super Fans. Just by signing up, they are telling you that they are already interested in what you have to say. Give them some exclusive content in exchange and make them feel special. You will keep people on your list—and they'll keep coming back.

Chapter 10

To Blog or
Not to Blog

It's none of their business that you have to learn to
write. Let them think you were born that way.
Ernest Hemingway

Developing a personal brand online is crucial to your success
as an author, and blogging is a critical element of that plan.
I know it's not always easy to find the time, and sometimes
it seems so irrelevant compared to your other priorities. Almost every one of my clients moans when I mention blogging.
Usually they have just finished writing the book and the last
thing they want to do is to write more. Some of my clients
are CEOs of large companies, and others are masters of the
universe in their fields, and I am almost embarrassed to ask
them to take time out of their busy days to blog. One of my
favorite responses came from a client who is a neurosurgeon.
When we started talking about blogging, he started to laugh

and then asked if he should save someone's life or write a blog. It's all relative, isn't it? Thankfully, our doctor loved to write and found it relaxing.

Why you should blog

If you are asking, "What's in it for me?" or "Why should I invest time blogging?" you should know that blogging brings traffic to your site, it showcases your expertise, and it helps you stand out from the crowd. After all, there is no competition for you.

Although blogging may not provide instant gratification, it should be viewed as an investment in your career, brand, and future. I wish I could tell you that every time you blog, tons of people will read that blog entry and share it. Unfortunately, that is just not the case. But every now and then we can hit it big with our blogs.

It happened to me. One of my blogs on MindBodyGreen went viral and has been shared over 44,000 times. It was a blog I wrote about the books that inspire me. I swear I wrote it in thirty minutes. You really never know which blog will resonate with your readers.

One year we represented and placed two of the most-shared blogs of the year on Facebook. It was a very exciting time. Author and client Lisa Bloom had written a book called *Think: Straight Talk for Women to Stay Smart in a Dumbed-Down World.* We had an opportunity to place a blog by her on Huffington Post called "How to Talk to Little Girls." The blog resonated with people and they began to share it. Within a few days it was shared 50,000 times on Facebook. At this writing, it has been shared by over 81,000 people on Facebook and had over 5,000 tweets.

The other author whose blog hit a nerve was Ron Clark, author of *The End of Molasses Classes: Getting Our Kids Unstuck, 101 Extraordinary Solutions for Parents and Teachers.* He wrote a blog called "What Teachers Really Want to Tell Parents." We were able to place it on CNN.com, and to date it has been shared over a million times on Facebook alone.

Both of these books became *New York Times* bestsellers shortly after the success of these blogs. That success was not only due to the blogs, but the popularity of the blogs certainly didn't hurt!

You may not have the contacts to get your blog on CNN. com, but LinkedIn and Medium have opened the doors to everyone. You should still blog on your own site for the SEO and traffic benefits, but there is no harm in posting your blogs elsewhere for added exposure.

Blogging is a gateway to building your personal brand. Each blog offers you the opportunity to share your knowledge and expertise, and build a following. With a little bit of focused effort, a plan, and allotted time, you can become known as an expert or thought leader in your industry.

 Tip for #BusyAuthors

"Those who tell the stories rule the world."
Native American proverb

Keep your goals and brand in mind as you begin to shape your blogging plan, and remember that blogging is the foundation of content for your website.

Blogging checklist

Writing blogs can be distracting, an unproductive time sink. There—I've just listed most of the arguments against blogging. Now let me make my case. Being an author today is like being a small business owner. You need a marketing strategy or you will go out of business. If people can't find you, they can't buy your books. You have many choices when it comes to marketing, but I consider blogs (like websites) a key part of the foundation of a digital strategy.

☐ **Blogs are the absolute best way to drive traffic to your websites.**
For book authors in a competitive marketplace, the need to blog couldn't be clearer. Blogs position authors as experts and thought leaders. Blogs give authors the opportunity to stay connected with their readers and build their online community. Rick Dragon, the CEO and cofounder of DragonSearch, a digital marketing agency, says, "The best tactic we've deployed to consistently increase traffic to websites is blogging. This isn't about writing another blog post—it means writing really valuable and relevant content."

☐ **Blogs are a natural extension of you as a writer.**
Consider the time you spend blogging as an extension of your job as a writer. Sure, the publisher will offer support and expertise, but to communicate with your readers 24/7 (which is now the expectation and the norm) you need to develop different types of content. Blogging is a great way to share your knowledge, test how your content reso-

nates, and collaborate with others. Blogs also provide you with the opportunity to link your content to your books, ebooks, white papers, audio recordings, slide presentations, videos, and webinars, so there are lots of cross-promotional opportunities.

☐ **You can showcase your expertise and define your niche.** Every blog you write helps define your personal brand. You can position yourself as the go-to expert in your field. Developing your personal brand takes time, but as you continually contribute content in your niche, you will connect with and identify your ideal audience. You can position yourself to promote more books, as well as apps, conferences, videos, your website, and more. When you become known as an expert in a field, you also become more valuable to publishers and agents.

☐ **Keep it interesting.** One consideration here is to be flexible with the topics of your blogs. You certainly don't want to blog about things that are not related to your book topic, but you can have some flexibility. For example, I usually blog about book marketing, but last year I posted two completely unrelated blogs, one on gratitude and the other a personal one on living wholeheartedly. Believe it or not, both of those blogs bring more traffic to our site than any other. Go figure.

☐ **You can write your next book.** Yes, creating your next book is not as easy as stringing together a collection of your blogs, but it's much easier to write a 700-word blog than it is to type out a 50,000-word book. Since big projects are more easily accomplished in small bites, view your blog writing as a laser-like focus on creating the chapters of your next book, one chapter at a time. The act of writing your blogs might point you in a different direction for your next book project based on what topic resonates the most with your audience.

☐ **Blogs can be evergreen content.**
You can write about topics that are still relevant years from now. Once your book is written, you can slice and dice sections of your book to create blogs. You can repurpose old content with updated links, incorporating new trends and a fresh perspective.

☐ **Blogs build relationships.**
By giving them valuable content, you are investing in your relationship with your readers. Your blog can be one of the most effective strategies for reaching people, and it can grow your readership or subscriber base. You can find readers who are interested in your subject, build anticipation for your book, network with others in your field, establish a foundation for your social media marketing, and showcase your value by letting readers sample your content. Online branding with a blog is no longer a luxury or an afterthought — it is a necessity. And it can be quite fun!

► **Tip for #BusyAuthors**

When considering your content strategy (meaning what to post), try to make sure that your content entertains, informs, and delights your readers! Always be generous with your knowledge and you will discover that it has a bounce-back effect, particularly in the world of social media.

Create a marketing calendar

Creating a marketing/editorial calendar is similar to organizing your book by chapters. You create an outline and know what information goes into each chapter and what information is coming. An editorial calendar is a scheduled pipeline of editorial content, and there are several good reasons to create one for your content generation work.

Editorial calendars keep you organized. You can see what topics you will be writing about and keep your content varied. You can schedule your content to lead your readers naturally to a call to action, like contacting you for work or purchasing your book.

A calendar will keep you on track and on deadline. It can also highlight gaps in your content or show when you are repeating content. Make sure you are providing content of value in your niche and that your content is varied.

Calendars identify themes and potential integrations with other elements, such as email and videos. Depending on your particular niche, you may want to write content that is seasonal and timely for a certain time of the year. Editorial calendars allow you to think about what people are interested in at different seasons and write content customized for those interests and time period.

The next page shows a simple example. You'll want to customize this approach for your readers and your industry.

Month	Holidays/ Events	Newsletter	Blog Topic	Social Media	Promote
Jan	New Year MLK Birthday	Wishes for the new year news from the industry link to new blog update on the book	5 ways to make this year your best MLK and his impact on my writing Volunteering for MLK Day	Inspirational quotes for the New Year and MLK Photos from your day of service Post your New Year's resolution	Update on the book. Title survey or ask for advice on the book jacket.

 Tip for #BusyAuthors

50 percent of the US population is on the East Coast, so be sensitive to that fact when you are setting up themes for your calendar. If most of the country is buried in snow, you don't want to be giving people advice for summer fashions even if you live some place warm.

Content ideas

While it's easier to reach people online, you have a lot of competition for their attention. Here are some content ideas:

1. Tell stories. People remember stories more than any other type of content. Even if you have a lesson to share, wrap that lesson up in a story.
2. Get to the point quickly. No one is going to read three paragraphs to discover your point.
3. What questions do your readers ask you? Turn those questions into blog posts.
4. Ask yourself if the content you are writing provides value to your audience.

5. Be a resource provider. Offer solutions, tips, techniques, and strategies.
6. Mix it up and post different types of blogs: Consider guest posts, interviews with other experts in your niche, and research-based posts.
7. Numbered lists are very popular so you may want to consider writing 5 Ways to ...
8. Write book reviews and tag the authors.

We've talked content and schedule; now let's talk about putting those beautiful finishing touches on your blogs with relevant images.

Selecting photos and images for your content
Beautiful images capture the attention of your readers. Carefully selected photos can encapsulate your brand. Every blog you write should have an image or multiple images for each post.

Stock photography and royalty-free photography are great options for authors writing blogs and not wanting to break the bank ordering photos. Using stock photography ensures that you have permission to use the photos you are ordering and that you stay clear of any copyright infringement. Speaking of that, it's best to refrain from using images you find on Google Images because you need written permission to use them from the owner of the photo or the copyright holder. Many Google images are copyrighted or trademarked.

(This information will be a little dated by the time you see it, but I still wanted to include it. I will update this list on my website, www.fauziaburke.com.)

iStockphoto.com. You can create an account and search for photos using keywords. Buy iStockPhoto Credits or a subscription—whatever is most cost-effective for you based on the frequency of your posts—and buy your images. You can use the iStock Lightbox feature as a place to store images you like for future use.

Shutterstock.com. Shutterstock is a provider of digital imagery licensing, operating in more than 150 countries and 20 languages.

Gettyimages.com. Getty Images has one of the biggest databases of stock media, especially for premium, conceptual, high-resolution images. Don't want to pay a small fortune per photo? You now can select Getty images with an embed tag on the image, allowing you to place a photo on your website, blog, or social media channel free of charge. When someone clicks the image, they will go to Gettyimages.com. This is a cost-effective alternative. Keep in mind that Getty reserves the right to remove images from its free library at any time.

With your content creation through text and images, always aspire to make your readers' lives easier and more enjoyable by answering their questions, entertaining them, solving their problems, and aiming to be the go-to information source for your industry. Stay on top of trends. It's a winning formula for building your personal brand with your community of loyal readers.

► **Tip for #BusyAuthors**

Okay: We have our goals and we've gotten organized. You've done a lot of hard work! Take a break. Go for a walk, meditate, cook, garden—do anything fun. Put this book away, step away from your computer or anything digital. It is important during this process not to burn out or get overwhelmed. After all, you need to be fresh for your next dive into social media and social networking.

Chapter 11

Social Media and Social Networking

*No matter what your pursuit, the most
fulfilling part is sharing it with others.*
Eli Broad

Social media allows you to have conversations with your readers, and it will be a big part of your online marketing strategy. Ages ago I wrote an article on Huffington Post called "It's 2010: You Really Need to Be on Facebook." As you can imagine, that was a bit controversial. In fact, Donna Fenn, author of *Upstarts*, wrote on her blog that judging by the response, you'd think that I had asked people to walk around naked. That was many years ago, and I can't tell you how often I still hear authors say, "All people do on social media is discuss what they ate for breakfast." Only people who are not on social networks say that, since for the rest of us social media has become an important way to stay connected with friends, colleagues, and readers. It is surprising that anyone could still deny the benefits of social media for marketing, but I am still having those conversations.

More often than I can count, I talk with authors who start out saying, "Social media is stupid." Many of my clients join social media kicking and screaming, but once they are on a network they love it. None of my clients has ever said, "Why did you do this to me? I want out." Not one. So if you have been sitting on the sidelines, I encourage you to try social media before you dismiss it. Once you are on social media you will see the benefits of having a presence there.

Just remember that your goal with social media is to build engagement. Once an author reached out to me on Facebook and said, "My publisher said I have to be on Facebook to sell books, so here I am." Unfortunately, it's not good advice, because Facebook won't help you sell books. Not in the one-post, one-sale way. So if that is the only reason you joined Facebook, you'll soon feel frustrated.

Before we jump too deeply into the social media chapter, I want you to know that I understand (more than most) the value of social media. However, I also know that there is a price we pay for being distracted. No amount of social media is going to help you sell a book that is not well written. So remember to keep things in balance and focus your time and energy strategically. I know some people who are always on social media, and I am not sure there is an upside to focusing so much of your time and talents on social media. Heed your mom's advice: "Everything in moderation."

As you get serious about your social media strategy you'll need to make an investment of time up front to learn these tools and figure out what to say and what works. But after you've done that, don't lose yourself in chasing "Likes."

So why spend time on social media?

Social media provides us with the tools to listen and to see what is important to our audience. It helps us learn and engage and bond with people we have never met. For me, seeing pictures of my friends' kids growing up right before my eyes makes me happy. It helps me connect with potential clients and also keeps me involved with clients I worked with years ago. There is no other way to be so personally involved in the lives of my clients. Social media allows me to learn from people who are smarter than I am. I look at their feeds to see what they are reading and what conferences they are attending. It's like having multiple mentors at the same time. Social media has allowed me to connect, engage, and be more effective.

 Tip for #BusyAuthors

Listen to your community. Successful branding is a two-way street.

Important information

Before we jump into specifics, here's an important distinction to remember. You may think social media and social networking are interchangeable terms that mean the same thing, but they are actually quite different. Social media is the content you create in any form—whether that's a blog, video, podcast, slideshow, newsletter, or social media post. Social networking is about the relationships you form as a result of social interactions on different platforms and sites. Social networking is all about the act of engagement—creating relationships, communicating with your readers, and building a following.

Your social media strategy will determine what content you will create and share, and your social networking strategy will build your relationships by interacting and creating conversations. You need a strategy for both content sharing and engagement.

I also want to say that it is challenging to cover everything about every social network in this short book. I've tried to cover essential strategy here. If you need help signing up and learning these networks, I would suggest asking for help from a family member or friend. There are also lots of free blogs and videos available online, and of course there are many books on these topics. I hope I can give you just enough information here to make you dangerous. (Just kidding.) But I do hope you'll get interested and excited so you can see the value of these networks and how they fit into your online marketing strategy.

 Tip for #BusyAuthors

The key word in social media is *social*. Keep in mind that it takes time to build a following, so have patience and don't expect results overnight.

There are many social networks these days, and you can engage in as many as you want. But if you are struggling to keep up with them, I suggest you start with LinkedIn, move onto Facebook, and then check out Twitter. These are the most popular social networks. However, you may find that you enjoy Instagram more than Twitter or Pinterest more than Facebook. It's totally okay to ditch networks you don't like for others you like better.

Just remember the work you did on knowing your readers and then match the network where your readers hang out. A September 2015 study by Reality Mine shows some general trends:

- Facebook is overall the most popular site.
- Image-sharing sites (like Instagram) are mainly preferred by Millennial women.
- Women are five times more likely to use Pinterest than men are.
- Twitter is the only social media channel to be used by men more than women in every generation.
- The most common income bracket among social media users is $50,000 to $74,999.
- Twitter users are most likely to be educated to bachelor's degree level.
- Social media users are relatively well educated. Pinterest users are more likely to have a graduate degree, while nearly 30 percent of Twitter users have at least a bachelor's degree.

LinkedIn

LinkedIn is the most professional of the social networks, and it's the easiest to use. Not all social networking venues are created equal. Each has its own identity, and what works on Facebook and Twitter may not work on LinkedIn. While you can use all social media platforms for an integrated approach to marketing your book and other products and services, you have to know your audience for each platform. The LinkedIn audience is where professionals connect and help each other to be effective, productive, and successful.

LinkedIn gives you the opportunity to showcase your professional experience. It is a great way to gain more visibility, increase your rank with search engines, and inform your professional network about your book. To use LinkedIn effectively, your communication should therefore be professional. This is not the place to post pictures of your pets or beach vacations.

Here's a checklist to get you started on LinkedIn:

☐ **Complete your profile.**
It's really important to fill the LinkedIn profile as completely as possible. Your headshot is very important on LinkedIn because a professional contact may remember your face but not your name. When you send someone a request to link, they'll notice your face first.

☐ **Stay professional.**
If you wouldn't put it on your resume or in your portfolio, or say it in an interview, don't put it on your LinkedIn page. It's not the forum for personal posts or any type of oversharing.

☐ **Connect carefully.**
It's more effective to form relationships just as you would in person. Don't reach out and ask to connect professionally with people you don't know. Work relationships slowly through shared connections or referrals.

☐ **Share resources.**

On LinkedIn, be sure to share articles, stories, and resources that will help those in your network. Avoid posting only your own content.

☐ **Build your credibility.**

Work on building up your recommendations, but avoid just swapping recommendations with people you know since that doesn't look very authentic. Make sure you have at least some recommendations on your LinkedIn page.

☐ **Stick with professional photos.**

Use a professional photo of yourself. First impressions count.

☐ **Don't ask for favors.**

Nothing is more annoying than a person asking for favors on LinkedIn before they have built a relationship with the other person. LinkedIn, like in-person networking, is about give and take. Always give first.

☐ **Don't send mass emails.**

Connecting with people is a privilege. LinkedIn is best for one-to-one communication. It is not a forum for mass email announcements. If you plan on announcing your book, webinar, or event, be selective.

☐ **Update your LinkedIn status.**

Be mindful of sharing information related to your areas of expertise and content of value. You want to find the right mix of sharing and promoting.

☐ **Add links.**

Link up your website, blog, Twitter feed, and other social media accounts to your LinkedIn account. You have space for other URLs, and you can customize the link text.

☐ **Give endorsements.**

LinkedIn allows you to endorse the skills of others. Be generous and endorse others for their great work.

☐ **Provide answers.**

Join groups relevant to your industry and/or the topic of your book and be helpful.

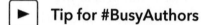 **Tip for #BusyAuthors**

I use LinkedIn to find people before **every** phone call and meeting. If it's appropriate, I send them an invitation to say: "I look forward to talking with you tomorrow. Until then, please join my professional network on LinkedIn." It's a great way to learn about people, and it shows that I am curious and attentive. It's also a good way to encourage them to look at my profile so they can see my experience and skills.

Facebook

I know some people have problems with Facebook, from security and privacy issues to a sense that it is not effective for marketing. I feel differently. Facebook has more than a billion users, and it is no exaggeration to say that you are at a great disadvantage without a Facebook author page. Engaging with your readers on Facebook can build your brand, establish your presence, increase your email list, and lead to increased book sales and other business opportunities.

If you are only on Facebook because you want to sell something, I am not sure any social networking will really work for you. Facebook allows us to connect with our readers, but we need to respect and invest in these relationships, always offering value. Do it right and you can build a community around your book and promote your book at the same time.

Your profile will help you attract the right type of people. If you are interested in politics or arts or business, share those interests because like-minded people will respond to you. Our profiles make us approachable and easy to relate to.

Facebook creates a platform and a community of savvy consumers connecting with friends, family, coworkers, and acquaintances to share advice, information, and recommendations. More than 30 billion pieces of content such as web links, news stories, blog posts, videos, and photo albums are shared each month. Facebook is thus one of the most important social media platforms for marketing and communication. I know that not everyone shares my opinion, but I have seen the benefits for my clients and myself firsthand.

And clearly Facebook isn't going anywhere. People on Facebook read books and tell their friends and colleagues about them. As an author, engaging on Facebook allows you to be closer to your fans and prospective readers, and a Facebook author page is a must-have. Here's a checklist to guide your first steps on Facebook:

☐ **Be authentic.**

   Who is your reader? Remember, you are posting to build a community of people who are interested in your book and brand. Always post for your audience while making sure that what you post is congruent with your brand. Refer back to earlier chapters where you answered questions on your brand identity and reread your brand statement.

- ☐ **Share and connect on your About you page.**

  Optimize your About page. Share a short bio and include links to your website to help drive traffic from Facebook to your website. Add a simple "Connect with me on my blog here" and add a URL to link them.

- ☐ **Always offer value.**

  Use your Facebook business page to make some deposits in your relationships by being social and helping others. Post helpful status updates with your expert tips, share something interesting you have read, or make comments on other people's posts. Don't disappear when you have nothing to promote.

- ☐ **Engage with your fans.**

  Many studies show that friend recommendations are the most reliable driver of purchasing decisions. You can ask a favor from your network once you have invested in your relationships. Enlist fans (or family and friends) to help you promote your book. We all need help from our social and professional communities, and your friends and fans will be a lot more inclined to help if you already have an established relationship.

- ☐ **Keep your posts varied.**

  You don't want to be the author who just drops in blog links to your Facebook page. Think two-way conversation and interaction. Spark a conversation. Ask for feedback on something along with your blog post. It's tough to say what is the ideal number of posts you should make each day. Almost every year there is new information. The latest thought is that you should post once every two days. I am not sure I agree with that. To build a relationship you need to engage consistently. Test things out. Try posting until you land on the sweet spot. For many of my clients it's one to two times a day. Too many posts and people may unlike your page.

☐ **Pay attention to what works.**
This sounds like a no-brainer, but it's worth mentioning: Do more of what works. Check out Facebook Insights for ideas on what type of content works best and when.

☐ **Ask for what you want.**
Direct calls to action on Facebook are extremely effective. Just be selective. Ask your fans to share, comment, or like a post. Or simply say, "Chime in below!" You can ask your followers to share the news about your book or share an offer you created on your cover image. Or simply say, "I'd love to hear your feedback." When you ask your audience to interact, there is a better chance they will actually do it.

☐ **Post images.**
It sounds obvious, but images can increase engagement and sharing on Facebook. Use a profile photo that looks professional. Remember your brand goals here. Select a cover photo that matches your website and brand voice. Shorter posts are more popular.

☐ **Ask yourself: Will this be shared?**
This is an excellent filter to run your content through before posting. If it is likely to be shared, make sure you have branded it with your tagline, website colors, or website URL.

☐ **Show useful information.**
Give a tip, bit of advice, inspiration, free ebook, or quick video to instantly position yourself as an expert by of-

fering valuable content without asking anything of your readers. Giving builds trust with your audience.

☐ **Run a Facebook ad or promoted post.**
Promoted posts can give your popular posts an even bigger boost. While there are many different types of Facebook ads to run, ads and promoted posts can significantly increase your followers.

► **Tip for #BusyAuthors**

Post content that entertains, educates, or inspires. Here are some ideas for content on Facebook besides links and photos: Find out more about your fans by asking questions. Use quotes from books you love. Post short thoughts or comments. Fill-in-the-blank posts usually get lots of engagement.

Obviously, my personal Facebook page offers more engagement and has more people than my author page. I use both of them in harmony. My personal page is for engagement, and my author page is for promotion. I try to apply the same respectful approach to both. Facebook Insights can be very useful and is only available for author pages. One good way to use Insights is to see where most of your fans are located, then consider adding those cities to your book tour.

Twitter

I have a confession to make: I was not an early adopter of Twitter. The charm of Twitter eluded me for that first year. I didn't get it. I didn't get the language. It seemed like a string of links to even more things I had no time to read. It felt overwhelming. Facebook made sense as a perfect extension of the networking I was already doing.

Sound familiar? I hear the same thing from many people. But what I discovered when I actually engaged on Twitter has turned me into a fan. Twitter has been one of the greatest learning tools of my career.

People on Twitter are generous with their time and knowledge. Yes, you will spend time on Twitter that you already don't have, but you will also learn things that will make you more valuable, smarter, and in the know.

If you are hesitant to join Twitter, you are not alone. I encourage you to give it a shot anyway. Set up an account, follow some people, and learn some things. Even if you don't plan to be very active, it is important to get a handle and follow others. It is a great platform to listen to others, chat about your book, and provide links to your blog posts, media events, and reviews—but only after you have built trust by promoting others and sharing valuable information.

The first thing to do on Twitter is to decide your goals for using Twitter:

- Is your goal to interact with the media or journalists?
- Do you want to gain exposure for personal branding in your area of expertise?
- Is it to learn from others who are experts in their field?
- Do you want to build your audience and email list?
- Or is your goal to increase traffic to your website and blog?

Your goal may include multiple objectives, but it's good to think about your Twitter goals so you can focus your efforts.

There's no need to panic if you don't have a ton of people following you right away. If you post good information, people will find you slowly and steadily.

The number of people on Twitter has increased every year since it launched. Some of the most popular activities on Twitter are sharing news in real time and sharing in group experiences like the Super Bowl or the World Cup. Here's a checklist for your experiments with Twitter:

☐ **Fill out your profile.**

When you sign up for Twitter, complete the profile as fully as possible. Add a photo, short bio, username, and real name. People want to know who you are. Your bio should include the title of your book. Make sure you include the URL for your website.

☐ **Observe.**

Spend your time just observing what others are doing before tweeting yourself. There are people you already follow (favorite authors, must-read columnists, magazines, newspapers, influential friends): just start following them on Twitter.

☐ **Be patient.**

At first, Twitter may seem overwhelming and difficult to use, but as you spend time on the network you will likely discover the benefits of sharing resources and collaborating with others. You have to invest some regular time on Twitter to build a community. As you work to become known as an expert in your niche, Twitter will help you establish your personal brand. Just don't expect instant success. Pace yourself and enjoy the journey.

☐ **Build your community.**

Be proactive and make a list of the people you want to get to know. Decide who you want to create relationships with and begin a conversation.

☐ **Share what you know.**

Start off by sharing your knowledge. I'll bet you know a lot about your industry and niche. Think of Twitter as a great way to share that information. If you read something helpful, share the link on Twitter and let others benefit from your find. Generosity is a good business practice.

☐ **Be a good community member.**

A good rule of thumb is to have a four-to-one ratio for self-promotion—one self-promotional tweet to four that will help others or engage the community through reply or retweet. Be polite. Remember that everything you say reflects on your brand and brand promise.

☐ **Support others.**

Whether it's experts in your space or media contacts, Twitter is a great way to learn from others. Initiate contact by retweeting the content of others to help support and promote them and foster good relationships. Remember not to ask people to follow you or to retweet you—just offer value, and relationships will happen naturally. If you read something you like on Twitter, retweet it. It's a great way to give credit to people who are putting out good information. If you want to join the conversation, use Reply.

☐ **Study the competition.**

Twitter is an open forum for you to study other people who might be in your field of expertise. See what they are doing and what's working for them and modify those tips for yourself to help market your book.

☐ **Add a hashtag.**

Use a hashtag for your book title to keep track of the conversations related to your book. It's also a good idea to join the conversation of a popular hashtag in your niche.

► **Tip for #BusyAuthors**

While tweets can only be a maximum of 140 characters, write tweets that are less than 120 characters so people have room to retweet your tweets and comments. Don't go overboard on using hashtags, since they can be #hardtoread and #distracting. Two hashtags should be your limit.

Pinterest

You may think of Pinterest as a place where scrapbooking fans, foodies, home interior aficionados, and fashionistas go to hang out online and share images, but Pinterest is a social networking site that can be used for so much more. Pinterest is now a marketing tool for businesses and authors. Depending on your readers, having a Pinterest page can raise brand awareness, increase traffic to your website, and drive purchasing decisions. Before you write off Pinterest as a craft-y outlet you don't have time for, consider that Pinterest can be used as a social media marketing tool to help promote you and your book, and that it's fun and easy to use.

If you aren't yet familiar with Pinterest, it's a social media platform where you can visually share web pages, photos, images, graphics, and videos by pinning them to online bulletin boards that you create. Most people with Pinterest pages develop themed boards to comprehensively cover their niche or areas of interest. What better way to identify and connect with your ideal audience than through your shared interests? Think of Pinterest as a lifestyle platform for your brand. Here's a checklist to help get started on Pinterest:

- [ ] **Maximize your Pinterest profile.**
  Make sure you fully fill out your profile with a compelling image that represents you and your brand. Include a description of you that makes people want to know more. Include an image of your book. Connect your Pinterest page to your website so your visitors can easily click through to it.
- [ ] **Create interesting boards.**
  Create boards on your Pinterest page in themed categories for things you and your target audience like. Pinterest can be great for novels. For example, if your novel is based in a particular country or part of the country or a particular time period, you can collect links and images to represent that time and place.
- [ ] **Start pinning.**
  Pinterest is the place for visual creativity. Pin up photos of your book, well-designed quotes, and video trailers of your book, or invite other people to share photos related to reading your book.
- [ ] **Pin your tour.**
  You can have a board about your book tour and pin the sites of bookstores and other venues that are hosting you. You can have a board where you pin all the great reviews

about your book. The ideas are endless, and remember that it's just a fun, graphic way to curate information.

☐ **Follow cool people.**
Use Pinterest to make connections. Begin by following interesting people within your niche. If you regularly interact with their Pinterest boards, they are likely to take notice of you and follow you back.

☐ **Make following easy.**
Add the Pinterest Follow Me button to your website and your other social media platforms. You can encourage people who go to your website, Facebook, and Twitter pages to join you on Pinterest as well.

When your readers know and like you as an author, they want to know what you like. Pinterest can help you grow a following by connecting with others through your similar interests. Tell your story and express your goals and brand voice through your Pinterest boards in creative ways.

▶ | **Tip for #BusyAuthors**

I use Pinterest to organize information in one place, including information that inspires and educates me; recipes and favorite restaurants; and infographics on marketing and small business trends.

What about Goodreads, YouTube, Tumblr, Instagram, Snapchat, Periscope, etc.?

I wanted this book to be short, so I could not cover every network. As a busy author, you have to decide where to put your time and focus your attention. If you are already using other networks, then just monitor which one provides the best value (delivers engagement and brings traffic to your site) and which one you enjoy. Then focus on two or three at the most. It's better to build a good community in a few places than to have a small presence in many.

 Tip for #BusyAuthors
Double down on what's working and ditch what's not.

In my experience, LinkedIn, Facebook, Twitter, and Pinterest bring the most traffic to an author's website. Building your social media network takes time, but you already have the expertise, and social media platforms are free. Once you know your readers and gain their trust, you will be able to promote not just your books but also your apps, conferences, videos, webinars, websites, online courses, and more (oh yes, they are all coming).

Chapter 12

DIY Online Book Publicity

To amplify your message and grow the reach of your brand and book you'll need to consider publicity. If you are working with a publisher they will provide publicity support, but it's also a good idea to consider options to augment their campaigns. There are two ways to go about getting attention in the media: One is to hire experts to help you reach the media, and the other is to do the legwork yourself. I'll be honest: Publicity is not rocket science. If you are committed to the process, you can do it yourself. It will take you longer and you will certainly spend many hours chasing opportunities, but you'll save money. When you hire a PR expert, you are hiring them for their time, expertise, and contacts. Unfortunately, results are not guaranteed. Trust me: That fact is as frustrating for us in the field as it is for you.

There's another thing to consider, and this may be difficult to hear: If you are self-publishing your book, you will probably get fewer reviews than if you were published by an established publisher. This is simply the truth. I totally understand the reasons to self-publish, but it's important to be aware of the implications of that decision on your publicity prospects. It definitely means that you'll have to focus more time on guest blogging and interviews.

Choosing the right public relations firm for your book

If you decide you want to hire a PR firm for your book, here are some important considerations:

1. **Know your needs and goals.** Before you begin your search, think about your PR goals. What is it that you want? Do you want to be on TV? Do you want reviews in newspapers? Or do you want to build exposure online? Whom do you want to reach? Do you know your target demographic? How long do you want to work with a PR agency? Do you want to work with a PR agency for a one-time book or project or for multiple projects longer term? Once you identify your goals, you'll be able to find an agency that can help you achieve them.

2. **Get a referral.** Your search should always start by asking your agent, publisher, or fellow authors for referrals of people they have worked with to get some names to begin the process. You can compare and contrast the agencies you consider and find the one that's the right fit. You can also work the process backward and find a successful book that's in the same realm as your book, and then find out what PR firm that author used.

3. **Do your research. Look up the agency online.** Check out their website and social networks as well as their current and past projects and testimonials. Find out how long they have been in business and what types of people they work with. In our connected age, it's easy to do your homework ahead of time to be able to narrow down your list based on your research. Make sure the agency you select is connected in the social media world. If they are connected digitally, they will be able to help promote and advise you in the social media space.

4. **Reach out and make contact.** Begin contacting several firms to pick the one that is right for you. Collect information on prices, timelines, and availability. Find out more about their area of specialty and expertise. Make sure your book is the type of book the PR agency does an effective job promoting. Now you can narrow your list further.

5. **Set up an interview.** Once you've narrowed down your list based on your budget, goals, and timing, you should set up an interview with each PR firm by phone or in person. A good firm will want to talk with you as well to make sure the fit is perfect. They should also encourage you to talk with other PR firms. Before you schedule the interview, give the firm the opportunity to learn about your book so you can hear their ideas and decide if you like what you are hearing. Ask questions just as if you are interviewing someone for a job. Find out the publications and media outlets where they have built relationships. Remember that a good PR agency should have an established network of media contacts. Make sure the agency you are talking to understands your brand. You can even request

a preliminary proposal of how they would go about publicizing your book. Good PR agencies have strong track records.

6. **Make the decision.** The most important part of your decision process should really be your instincts. It's all about knowing and liking the PR agency you are going to work with, because if you don't like the person initially, you will most likely be dissatisfied in the long run. Did you establish rapport upon initial contact? During the interview phase, which firm stood out? What agency do you like, respect, and trust the most? In the end, go with your gut and you will make the best decision for you and your book.

Along with results, a good PR agency should give you valuable information for building your brand and amplifying the exposure you are getting. In the end, it is all about the collaboration, so pick your team carefully.

DIY publicity

If you decide you want to do the publicity work yourself, focus on the Internet. Traditional media (newspapers, magazines, TV, radio) require great contacts and long lead times. In either case, before jumping in please read a book or take a course on the topic. It's easy to make mistakes, and you certainly want to avoid those when it comes to publicity.

What I can tell you is that as a busy author, online publicity will be a lot more effective for you. Online publicity, however, is not for everyone. It takes patience and a thick skin, since you may face rejection and silence. Authors often ask me what is the top website for generating sales. It's a legitimate question, but the answer is not necessarily obvious. In my experience, there is no single site that generates sales for every kind of book. Because the web is so segmented, different sites impact different books, so it all depends on your audience. One of our clients asked us to reach out to sushi sites to help promote his novel. When I asked him why, he said, "Because Katty [the main character] loves sushi." Now that may seem reasonable, but have you ever seen a sushi site featuring a novel just because the main character liked sushi? Probably not.

Another client asked us to get his book featured on the homepage of gap.com. "*The* gap.com? The people who make jeans?" I asked, confused. He said, "Yes, because their customer is my demographic." This may seem like a creative idea, but have you ever seen a book on the homepage of gap.com? Probably not.

Your time is limited and the Internet is vast, so try to manage your expectations. If something has never been done before, it's probably a long shot. So the first order of business is to make a list of websites and blogs on your wish list. It's okay to dream here and list the *New York Times*, but you also need to have a realistic list. Remember the work you did in earlier chapters on readers, goals, and dreams. It's worth looking at it again to help focus your attention on what you can achieve. The first thing to do is to build a list of websites and blogs that cover your topic. Note their URLs, social media feeds, and any contact information. Just remember your audience, which is often not as big and general as you may think. Pull out your work on Know Thy Reader. It will help you narrow your efforts.

When authors come to me and say, "I want to reach book bloggers or mommy bloggers," I often have to tell them that bloggers have very specific tastes, and these tastes are more specific than they may realize. For example, when reaching out to mommy bloggers, it is really important to know the age of their kids. Pitching a teen parenting book to a mommy blogger with a baby won't get you far. Pitching a sci-fi novel to a blogger who loves historical romances won't work either. Sending a World War II book to a blogger who covers the Civil War will make for a cranky blogger, and sending a press release to the wrong person may actually get you blacklisted. So if you want to take on this work, please approach it carefully and diligently. A misstep can be damaging for your brand, and unfortunately Google has a long memory.

Once you've made your list, you'll need to write a pitch. I know it's counterintuitive, but I hate press releases. They never really work for us. I find that having a conversation is a much better way to get the attention of the person on the other end. If you have done your research, it will be a lot easier to pitch the blogger and editor with something specific. It's better to pitch fewer people individually than pitching hundreds of people in one mass email.

Online publicity checklist

☐ **Search for blogs.**

If you are looking for bloggers to review your book, look for the ones who have already reviewed books. One of the ways you can narrow your search is by doing a Google search for a competing book. If you only search for the name or title, too many things will come up and it will be a chore to figure out which ones are reviews. However, you can do a Google search for the author's name or book title in quotes and the phrase "book review" or "interview," and you will get much more refined search results—for example, "Brene Brown" "Daring Greatly" "Book Review."

☐ **Know their beat.**

The best piece of advice to any author trying to build a relationship with bloggers is to build it through mutual respect, trust, and consistency. Make sure you know the blogger's focus and area of interest.

☐ **Work with a range of bloggers.**

It's good to know how much traffic a blog has, but don't dismiss bloggers with less traffic. It is important to look at the full reach of a blogger. Sometimes blog features from smaller blogs can generate more chatter on social networks. It's a good idea to follow them on Twitter, "Like" them on Facebook, and check out their social networks like Goodreads. Some bloggers post reviews on multiple sites so they can be more valuable for that reason alone. Remember also that placements on niche sites (those with less traffic) can sometimes be more effective than placements on a large general-interest site. You can work with bloggers who post reviews of your book, and those reviews can take on a life of their own. Reviews on sites like Twitter, Amazon, Barnes & Noble, Goodreads, LibraryThing, and Facebook all increase the search visibility of a book and its author. On these sites the reviews or features are all fluid and viral. They do not stay where they are created—they often take flight and have a much broader life than just the traffic on that original blog.

☐ **Make things easier.**

Understanding the needs of bloggers and online editors will help you work with them. Make note of the type of coverage they specialize in. Do they like to interview authors, review books, do raffles, or post guest blogs? Then make sure you send them the materials they need in a timely fashion. If you promise them a review copy of a book, send it quickly.

☐ **Approach bloggers one at a time.**

Every time I say that, people either roll their eyes in disbelief or try to sell me on the benefits of mail-merge mass email. But here's the honest truth: You are better off reaching out to 50 bloggers one at a time than to 500 via a mass email. You'll actually get better results. Is it time-consuming and labor-intensive? You bet. Is it worth it? Yes!

☐ **Don't push.**

Without follow-up nothing will come of your pitching, so you need to find time to follow up and develop skills in asking without being pushy or rude. Every good publicist masters the delicate art of begging.

☐ **Represent good content.**

Don't send out press releases, articles, or op-eds that are not written well. Make sure the content that leaves your hands always looks professional and does not have spelling or grammatical mistakes.

☐ **Be consistent and professional.**

There are a few endorsements from bloggers on our site, and I read them as market research for this book. Many noted that being consistent and professional is important to them. They also like it when you use their names.

☐ **Keep notes.**
All of these tips are fine, but unless you keep track of your research they'll be difficult to implement. At FSB, we have several fields in our custom-designed database that help us develop relationships with bloggers. We record when the contact was added, by whom, and any notes about their likes and dislikes. We also keep track of all the books sent to every blogger and which ones then featured our books. This practice allows us to learn more about the blogger with every interaction and send them only the books they would be inclined to cover. You can use a spreadsheet or database to keep track of your PR work. It's a good idea to keep thorough notes so you don't get confused about whom you've contacted and what the results were.

If you are doing your own publicity, consider developing an ongoing dialog and relationship with the bloggers. Share their information and be generous. Everyone appreciates a digital nod these days. Help them before you need their help.

Once you have searched for bloggers and pitched your book, you will need to wait for responses. If editors/bloggers request the book, your pitch is working. If not, you'll have to use another pitch. Try connecting your book to something in the news or a new study. When you do get a response, pounce on it. Attention is fleeting, and you don't want to wait. If the editor/blogger asks for a book or an interview, accommodate them right away.

Then in a couple of weeks follow up and make sure they got the book and ask if there is anything you can do to help. That's the cycle. It's not difficult. It's not rocket science. However, it requires lots of time and patience. Contacts with the media are worth so much because a publicist's relationship with an editor will boost your chances of getting a feature. If you are willing to put in the work, you can build the same contacts and relationships within your niche. It will just take some time.

Research tools

New tools show up all the time, and if I find a cool new one I will post it on my site at www.fauziaburke.com.

Social Mention. This site allows you to search an author, company, or topic across the web. You can get results from 100 social media sites in one place. My favorite part is that it gives you sentiment (positive, neutral, or negative) of the mentions all over the web, along with top keywords and top hashtags. It's handy.

TweetReach. This is one of my favorite sites. It allows you to search a topic, author, handle, or name and see how many people were reached by those tweets. You can also see who sent the tweets and how many followers they have. This is a helpful tool to search for people who have influence.

TwitterCounter. I love this site. It allows you to see the Twitter stats for any handle. You can see if the trend is for gaining followers or losing them. It also shows you how many tweets are made every day by any handle. TwitterCounter is useful for research and for monitoring the success of your Twitter feeds, especially if you have multiple accounts.

Google Trends. If you are working on a news topic, this is an excellent source because it gives you insights into the amount of traffic and geographic visit patterns.

Twazzup. This site allows you to filter news from live Twitter content. It's helpful to see trending topics and influencers for a given subject. It's better for searching topics than for an author's name.

Klout. One of the most popular Twitter research tools, Klout measures influence rather than just the number of followers. It's not without controversy, however, since many believe its metrics aren't accurate.

PR quick links

Alltop.com. This site has top stories and blogs on every topic imaginable. Pick the topics that relate to your book and check out curated information.

PR Daily from Ragan's. They have a great newsletter called *PR Daily* with tips and ideas.

HARO.com. Help a Reporter Out connects journalists on deadline with expert sources. It's a good idea to sign up for the free newsletter and then pounce on any opportunities you can. We have gotten some good hits from it.

Cision. This is a software program that offers media contacts. It's not cheap, but if you are willing to spend the money it's a great way to find up-to-date contacts.

Other ways to get publicity

I like online publicity, and I accept my bias, but don't ignore other ways to get attention. Just do the things that you enjoy:

- Look for trade association meetings, industry conferences, and conventions in your field and find opportunities to speak. You can submit a request to be a panelist or make a presentation. No matter what your field, there's likely a circle of influence you can tap into for connections and leads. Make sure you write up a speaker's page on your website highlighting the topics you speak about. Take photos and videos to turn the event into a multimedia opportunity to share on social media.

- One of the best ways to become known as an expert in your field is to host a free webinar and help other people. You can share tips and strategies and take questions from callers or questions posted on your website or through a conference call. Not only will you be helping people, but you can also promote your website, your social media sites, and your book.

- Use a variety of places (website, blog, social media) where you can post information, expand your features, publicize your book, and share your successes.

- Submit your blog to media outlets or other sites in your niche. The more eyes on your blog, the better. Each time your blog gets mentioned or posted, so does your name and the link to your website. Over time, this is the best way to increase the Google ranking of your site.

- Today people are looking for an authentic connection with you. Posting a video where you talk to your online community lets readers feel more connected to you. Video blogs are another way to share your expertise and passion and grow your digital presence.

- Reach out to niche communities for reviews and interviews, and write content for other sites so your name has better Google visibility.
- Social media is an excellent way to build relationships, but don't forget the value of face-to-face meetings, phone calls, handwritten notes, and emails. It's good to focus on important influencers, but leave room for accidental connections. Social media networking can be serendipitous—an online connection could lead to an important face-to-face meeting.
- Attend conferences for the opportunity to network, connect with other people, get referrals, and expand your network. You can promote yourself and your expertise with your business card and by following up after the conference is over. Remember to connect with your new friends in all your social media outlets.

All of these activities provide more exposure for your book and help to establish a strong digital footprint. My advice is to chat it up, be social, and continue building a social network. Build credibility and keep the lines of communication open.

 Tip for #BusyAuthors

The idea that you only promote your book during a narrow window around the publication date is an outdated concept. Today you should have a long-term strategy.

Phase 3
Staying the Course

Chapter 13

Promote Without Being Promotional

Heroes must see to their own fame. No one else will.
Gore Vidal

How people perceive you online can be very important in your branding. In your social networks, it's important to be likable and avoid rubbing people the wrong way. Someone once told me that there's a fine line between arrogance and confidence. I immediately thought: That's not true. There's a huge difference. I feel some people exemplify the difference perfectly. Malala Yousafzai is confident enough to talk with world leaders and ask them to change their policies. Yet she never seems arrogant.

Why is this important? It's an important distinction because we like working with confident people, but we don't like engaging with arrogant people. A UCLA study concluded that likable people ask questions, are genuine and honest, don't seek attention, and smile (among other things). These are easy things to do online and will go over better than being clever and snarky.

As the owner of a digital branding and publicity company, I know that perception is everything. If you seem confident, you'll thrive. If you seem arrogant, you'll alienate people. It's that simple and that important, so focus on being likable and sharing good information.

The best way to share good content is to refer to the work you did in phase 1. If you know your readers and what they need, your content will resonate with your audience. A good rule of thumb is to promote others more than you promote yourself. For example, in any given week you may want to share good content from other people and tag them. They may be inspired to return the favor. Be sure to pick the most relevant social media sites for you and your readers. If you try to be everywhere, you'll burn out.

Creating compelling content

If you are a published author, you've already done the hard part: You have written your book and had it published. There are all sorts of ways to use the content in your book to market yourself in the world of social media. Obviously, this is easier for nonfiction authors. However, novelists can also use some of these ideas.

If you peruse your book, you will easily see short sentences that pop out as quotable and are perfect for tweets. Look for those compelling quotes that showcase your expertise or fabulous writing and are less than 140 characters for Twitter. Find short quotes (120 characters) that people are likely to retweet. Create a hashtag using your book title each time you tweet to promote your book.

Facebook posts can be longer. You can create Facebook posts from quotes or use excerpts from your book. Snippets from your book that are helpful to others or inspire dialog among your Facebook followers make for ideal posts. You can also use the content of your book to write all sorts of tips. Tips are a great way to brand you as an expert because they are short, highly readable, and easily shared. When your Facebook followers share your tips, they are helping promote you and your book. If you have written a novel, you can help other authors write their own Great American Novel by providing inspiration and ideas.

To inspire more interest in your book or in you, create short lists that highlight your content. For example, if you wrote a cookbook you could write a short list entitled "Three Recipes You Can Try This Week" and use those three recipes to promote your entire cookbook. If your book is about leadership, write a short article on "Five Ways to Lead Your Team Through a Crisis." Articles that are written as quick, numbered lists appeal to people who are short on time but interested in your content. You can include a link to purchase your book and links to your social media sites within each article. Reach out to websites/blogs that are likely to share your lists (everyone needs content) and soon others will be helping you build your brand.

Each of the chapter headings in your book can be turned into blogs. Tease the content in your book by writing a shorter version of a chapter in blog form. It's a simple way to create a quick blog and tout your book with a sample of your content. Any stories you tell in your book or personal anecdotes you share can also make for compelling blogs. Be sure to always include a link to purchase your book in every blog you write. It's best to keep that link permanently in your bio.

Obviously, some of these ideas won't work if you are writing a novel, but you can adapt them for your own audience. You can write about the research you are doing or things you are discovering about your characters or yourself. You can interview other novelists or write about the challenges of writing a novel. Just remember to match the tone of your content to the tone of your book. If your book is fun and flirty, don't write blogs that are dark and sad. The idea is to attract likely readers.

All these ways will help you promote your book without feeling overly promotional. It takes a while to find your rhythm, and sometimes you will cross the line—but if you are being real and genuine and vulnerable, you'll be forgiven for any missteps.

 Tip for #BusyAuthors

The bottom line is this: Don't spam ever, on any network. Always show respect for others and their time.

Quality over quantity

Consistency is important in social media. In my experience, authors who post regularly (daily or several times a week) see higher engagement. Consistency builds brand recognition for companies and for people. If you keep showing up in my feeds, I will remember you.

Many of my clients complain about being a "content-generating machine." I understand their frustration. However, a little shift in attitude can make a big difference. First, it's important to think of the posts you make as conversations rather than announcements. Second, it is helpful to think of your community as family rather than people you never see. That little shift often enhances the quality of the posts for my clients and increases the level of engagement as well.

Although consistency is important, you really need to "show up" with good-quality information. Everything you do and say and post reflects on your brand. In any case, remember that a small, engaged community is much more valuable than a large number of followers. Respect and quality should be the cornerstone of your brand no matter what you write about.

Chapter 14

Monitor and Adjust

Efforts and courage are not enough without
purpose and direction.
John F. Kennedy

Like many things in life, planning is key for an effective strategy. View your online presence just as you already view important relationships—you have to check in, touch base, and give updates to keep your relationships going. So you don't just want to pop up randomly in the social media world and then disappear or go silent for a few months. To build your following you have to stay the course.

Monitor the data from your website, newsletter, and social networking, and adjust as you go. I am often asked what I know for sure in the book publishing, book marketing, and digital marketing industry. While there isn't one magic formula for every author and every book, there are some specific steps you can take to carve out your niche, build your brand, and create a community. Let's review them:

The age of the generalist is over. Find your niche, hone your skills, develop your audience, and be brilliant. Be a specialist. It's better to have deep knowledge of a narrow topic than to have shallow knowledge of a great many topics. It is easier to build a brand if you define your expertise and become the master of that niche. Maybe your audience will not be huge, but every person who needs that information will look to you first.

Don't wait. Start developing your brand and platform as soon as you have an idea for a book. It's never too early to create your audience and begin the conversations.

There is no everyone.com. Knowing your audience is essential for authors in so many ways. When you can easily describe your audience you can find them online. You can make your book better because you know exactly who you are writing for and how you can provide value. When someone tells you that you should do a Reddit AMA chat, you can say that that's not your audience. If you don't know your audience, you'll be spending time on activities that don't connect you with your readers.

Don't try to do everything. Just because something can be done online doesn't mean it should be done online. Don't try to keep up with every social media platform and app that is new or trendy. Think about your niche and what makes the most sense for you to do. Where do you think you can find your audience? Go there first. I always recommend that authors begin with a website because today's readers expect that at a minimum. Start your author website and make it about you first and your book second.

Approach people slowly and with respect. An email marketing blast can seem enticing when your time is limited and you have a long, overwhelming to-do list. But don't do it. It's better to take a few hours and write to one person at a time (to get a testimonial or to tell someone about your book or to pitch it to the media) than to do a mass email. I've tested this, and I know it to be true. You will get better results if you write one email at a time, even if it seems like a painstakingly slow process. Talking to people is a great privilege. Don't waste it. Sometimes we are all so busy and our heads so focused on the next meeting or work project that we don't appreciate the conversations we are having in the moment. Value every conversation and every person. That sounds like a cliché, but if it is one, that's because it's true: What you put into your relationships, you will get back.

You can't talk *at* people. You need to talk with them. You need to combine your social media efforts with social networking. Social media is what we create and upload. It is a one-to-many communication approach. Social networking is about interacting and listening, and it is successful when it's done peer-to-peer. Create content to share, but make sure you are creating conversations as well. You can't only post, you have to comment, read, listen, share, and go for connection. We all get caught up in social media numbers because it's like a game. How many Likes can I get? How many followers do I have? Watching your numbers grow can be an immediate-gratification pursuit, but truly it's better to have 1,000 engaged fans than 10,000 who don't care much about you. Go for interaction and deeper engagement.

Plan for the long game. The purpose of building your audience is to bring them along with you as you develop your projects. The feedback and encouragement you receive will make your book better. Use the questions you are asked as content ideas for your next blog post or chapter in your book. The questions your audience asks will give you insight into what your audience cares about most.

Sharing your expertise, ideas, and stories has never been easier, but building and keeping an audience has never been harder. Devote some time to your marketing plan daily and be patient. Results will happen.

How to protect your brand

In our socially connected world, our reputations have become global, making our brand, our name more important than ever. Social media has given us great ways to build our digital reputations. We have the ease of searching conversations, the ability to set alerts to help us monitor where and how often our names appear online, the constant availability of learning opportunities, and more ways to communicate and interact with others. All of these tools, which were not available just a few years ago, now make it possible for us to be proactive in maintaining, building, and protecting our good name.

Every month do a search on Google for your name in quotation marks. If I search for Fauzia Burke, Google will return all pages that have both Fauzia and Burke somewhere on the page. However, if I search for "Fauzia Burke" it will show the results for me, the pages where the two names appear together. If you have a common name, you may have to use your book title—for example, "John Smith" "Cook with Love." It is important to see what comes up on your first four search pages. The first page of a Google search result for your name is precious real estate. Most people don't go past two pages, but you should check the first four for your own name. Monitor your name every month and make sure that the information is not dated and reflects well on you. If there is a link you'd like to push further down in the search results, start blogging. New content, especially if it is popular, will push other content down. That won't happen overnight, but it will happen.

Setting your social media alerts (Google and/or Social Mention) is a great way to monitor your name and industry. If something important happens in your industry you'll know about it and can comment. If someone says something positive, a thank-you goes a long way. If there is negative chatter starting up around your name, alerts notify you right away and you can jump in and take care of things quickly. Alerts are not always reliable, so searching for your name every month is a useful fail-safe.

You are the guardian of your reputation. I know it is a big undertaking to build your personal brand and monitor it online, but the question to ask yourself is this one: If I don't invest in myself, why would anyone else?

Some Parting Advice

From my many years of promoting books online, the one thing I know for sure is that each book has its own sales trajectory. Some start selling right out of the gate and reach great heights, while others take the scenic route and sell steadily for years. And yes, there are some books that don't sell well at all. With the same marketing efforts, some books resonate with buyers better and more rapidly than others. Why is that?

As much as I would love to say, "I know the answer," it's just not possible to know. We have worked on many books that turned into huge bestsellers, and on many more that we wished would have sold better. What I do know for sure is that as publicists, we work with diligence and commitment. We believe in the books we promote. We are creative and flexible. We follow up religiously, and then we hope for a little magic.

When books don't sell as well as we had hoped, it is disappointing for everyone, not just their authors. The effectiveness of your online marketing efforts should not be judged by book sales alone. Through TV you can reach millions of people with one segment; this type of publicity is not possible online. Online exposure is diffused. You may get millions of hits, but they will be staggered. People will more likely come from different sites and see the information at different times, on different days, in different months or even years. When you think of online exposure, think longevity and message control.

Web features and links are available to readers now, and to new readers months and years from now. Like a snowball rolling down a hill, these features are able to grow thanks in large part to social media sites like Facebook and Twitter, which thrive on the constant sharing of information.

It is also amazing how well online placements translate into long-term visibility on Google. After checking on the long-term visibility of a successful book campaign we ran, I found forty links from a search of the author and book title, six months after the book was published. Of those links, twenty-four were from promotional activities. To my surprise and delight, 67 percent of the promotional links were web features. TV made up 4 percent; print, 13 percent; event promotion, 17 percent; and there were no radio links at all. In this case, it was clear that the web features had staying power. Also, most online features are directly linked to the bookseller, so making the step from liking a book to buying that book is just one click away.

The famous line said it all: "You gotta be in it to win it." If you are not available online when people are searching for information, the chances of them finding your book and buying it are slim. Remember: Every reader who takes the time to seek information on a related topic is an interested, committed, and qualified buyer—a warm lead. Just the kind we like.

Good luck, authors! Thank you for reading my book. Please reach out to me if I can help you succeed. If I've done my online branding job, you should be able to find me easily.

Acknowledgments

I want to offer a special thanks to the people I love the most: my husband and business partner, John Burke, whose love, intelligence, and ability to keep me grounded have been instrumental in my life. My daughters Syrah and Aliya, are the motivation for all that I do. Their courage and kindness is a source of daily inspiration and pride. My mother, Nuzhat Subhani, is my rock, and I am eternally grateful for her love and advice.

To my publisher, Berrett-Koehler, I am grateful to all of you for your support and spirit of collaboration. A special thanks goes to Kristen Frantz and Neal Maillet for championing my work.

Finally, I need to thank some book publishing people who gave me opportunities before I had earned them. To Greg Hamlin, who gave me my first contract in 1995 based solely on his faith in my abilities. To Raquel Jaramillo, whose friendship and encouragement has made a world of difference in my life. To Maggie Richards, Laurie Brown, Larry Kirshbaum, and

Bob Miller for putting my company on the map by trusting me with their most important authors during the early days of the web.

I am proud of my FSB team, Anna Sacca, Leyane Rose, and Courtney Allen, for their integrity, work ethic, and loyalty. They totally have my back, and that's a rare and wonderful thing. Thank you to my fabulous colleagues.

To all my clients, friends in book publishing, even people I have met only once at a conference, I thank you with all sincerity. I am better having known you.

Index

A

advertising, 45, 102
Alltop.com, 121
Amazon.com, 1, 66, 117
American Legion, x
Are You Fully Charged?
   (Rath), 38
Associated Press, 36
authors
   assessing current activities,
     52–55
   avoiding burnout, 3, 128
   building a personal brand, 1–2,
     7–14, 17, 42–45, 56, 81, 103,
     116, 127, 130, 136–37
   communicating with readers,
     2, 8, 37, 45, 82–83, 92, 95,
     127–28
   developing a priority list,
     42–47
   goal statements, 31–32
   goals for book, 28–33
   identifying audience, 21–24,
     134
   motivation, 16–17
   showcasing expertise, 29, 43,
     66–67, 80, 83, 97, 103, 122,
     123, 128–30
   understanding audience, 19–
     21, 36, 62, 83, 84, 93, 96, 99

B

Barnes & Noble, 66, 117
Beech, Mary, 10
Berg, Patty, 37
Berrett-Koehler Publishers, 37
bestsellers, xi, 61, 81, 139
blogs, blogging, x, 3, 43–44, 54
   blogging checklist, 82–84
   content, 83, 84, 86–87,
     128–30
   graphics for, 87–88
   importance of, 79–80
   to-do list for, 57
   working with bloggers, 115–19
Bloom, Lisa
   Think: Straight Talk for Women,
     80
bookstore tours, 66, ix
bookstores, 66

branding, 1–2, 7–14, 81, 103, 116, 127, 130, 136–37
Brite (conference), 10
Burke, Fauzia, ix, 136

C
CAN-SPAM Act, 74
Cision, 121
Clark, Ron
   The End of Molasses Classes, 81
CNN.com, 81
conferences, 123
Constant Contact, 53, 75
cookbooks, 129
Costanzo, Peter, 36
Crown Publishing Group, 37, 38

D
Daily Beast, The, x
demographics, 24–25
Dragon, Rick, 82
DragonSearch, 82

E
email lists, 66, 73–77, 135
   content, 76
   design of, 76
   software for, 75–76
   timing, 75–76
   tracking results, 76, 77
Empire of the Summer Moon (Gwynne), xi
End of Molasses Classes, The (Clark), 81

F
Facebook, xii, 55, 67, 80, 81, 92, 108, 109, 117, 129, 140
   advantages of, 98–99
   advertising on, 45

author pages on, 39, 44, 45
building a personal network on, 44–45
Facebook Insights, 101, 102
to-do checklist for, 99–102
Fenn, Donna
   Upstarts, 91
fiction, 128, 129
Frantz, Kristen, 37
FSB Associates, ix–xi, 119

G
gap.com, 115
GetResponse, 77
Gettyimages.com, 88
Godin, Seth, 8
Goodreads, 46, 55, 117
Google, 8, 63, 65, 87, 123
   searches, 44, 63, 65, 70–71, 116–17, 139–40
Google Analytics, 68–70
Google Trends, 121
Grafton, Sue, 61
graphics (*see* images)
Gwynne, S.C.
   Empire of the Summer Moon, xi
   Rebel Yell, x, xi

H
HARO.com (Help a Reporter Out), 121
hashtags, 106, 120, 129
History News Network, x
Huffington Post, x, 80, 91

I
iBooks, 66
images, 65, 66, 76, 87–88, 101, 106–7, 122
Indiebound, 66

Instagram, 24, 55, 67, 95
iStockphoto.com, 88

J

journalists, 103, 121

K

Kate Spade, 10
keywords, 70–72, 88, 120
Klout, 121

L

Levine Greenberg Rostan
    Literary, 36
LibraryThing, 117
LinkedIn, 55, 67, 74, 95–96,
    109
    building a profile on, 44
    to-do checklist for, 96–98
Lloyd, Kate, 37
lynda.com, 58

M

MailChimp, 53, 75
mailing lists, 3, 53–54
    developing an email newsletter,
        43, 76
    to-do list for, 57, 75–77
    tracking results, 76, 77
marketing
    advertising on social media,
        102
    developing a plan, 51–58, 135
    email blasts, 135
    marketing calendars,
        85–86
    mobile users, 65
    niche marketing, 8, 34
MindBodyGreen, 80

N

New York Times, 61, 62, 81, 115
nonfiction, 128

P

Pew Research, 25
pictures (*see* images)
Pinterest, 55, 67, 95, 109
    advantages of, 106–7
    Follow Me button, 108
    to-do checklist for, 107–8
PR Daily, 121
press coverage, 67
publicists and PR firms, x–xi
    hiring, 39–40, 111–14
    online PR to-do list, 116–19
publishers
    book promotion, x, 1, 37, 38, 40

R

Rados, Kate, 38
Rath, Tom
    Are You Fully Charged?, 38
    StrengthsFinder 2.0, 38
reader profiles, 21–24
readers
    connection with authors,
        8–9, 37, 61–62, 82, 122–23,
        127–28, 135
    creating an audience, 1–2,
        134–35
    developing conversations with,
        17–18, 36, 128–31, 135
Reality Mine, 95
Rebel Yell (Gwynne), x, xi
Reddit, 134
reviews
    soliciting, 116–18
Rostan, Stephanie, 36

S

Scribner/Simon & Schuster, 37
search engine optimization
    (SEO), 63, 71–72, 81
    SEO consulting firms, 71–72
search engines, 8, 44, 63, 65, 70,
    96, 123, 138–40
self-publishing, 111–12
    DIY publicity, 114–16
Sherman, Wendy, 38
Shutterstock.com, 88
SMART goals, 30
Snapchat, 55
social media, x–xi, 67
    alerts, 137
    content, 100–101, 118, 128–31
    demographics of, 24–25
    developing content for, 56–57
    engagement strategies, 3,
        122–23
    getting website traffic from, 55
    researching, 119–23
    sharing on, 101
    to-do list for, 58
    value of, 91–93
Social Mention, 120, 137
social networking, 24–25, 58, 67,
    70, 91–95
Squarespace, 63
StrengthsFinder 2.0 (Rath), 38
Super Fans, 3, 66, 73, 74, 77

T

television, 16, 21, 30, 67, 112, 114,
    140
testimonials, 67, 113, 135
*Think: Straight Talk for Women
    in a Dumbed-Down World*
    (Bloom), 80
trade associations, 122

Tumblr, 55, 67
Twazzup, 121
TweetReach, 120
Twitter, 45, 55, 67, 74, 95, 97, 108,
    109, 117, 128–29, 140, xii
    advantages of, 102–3
    to-do checklist for, 104–6
TwitterCounter, 120

U

Upstarts (Fenn), 91

V

value propositions, 30–31
video, 46, 122–23
    online courses, 58

W

Washington Independent Review
    of Books, x
web analytics, 67, 101
    bounce rates, 71–72
webinars, 122
websites, 52–53, 122
    building and updating, 42–43,
        134
    design of, 61–62, 63–64
    measuring website traffic, 57,
        67–70, 83
    redirection to website, 65
    referrals, 70, 122
    sales links, 129
    to-do list for, 57
Wendy Sherman Associates, 38
wix.com, 63
WordPress, 63

Y

Yousafzai, Malala, 127
YouTube, 55, 67

About the Author

Fauzia Burke is the founder and the president of FSB Associates, one of the first firms to specialize in online publicity and marketing for publishers and authors. Founded in 1995, FSB Associates has successfully launched more than 2,000 book publicity campaigns, many of them for bestsellers and award winners. FSB now has offices on both the East and West Coasts of the United States to better serve the needs of authors and publishers.

Fauzia started her career in the marketing departments of John Wiley & Sons and Henry Holt and has spent her entire professional career in book marketing and publicity. A sought-after online marketing expert, consultant, and speaker, Fauzia writes regularly for Huffington Post, MariaShriver.com, and MindBodyGreen. She is often a guest speaker at Book Expo of America and has presented at New York University, Macmillan Sales Conference, HarperCollins Sales Conference, the Association of American Publishers Annual Conference, Digital Book World, and the American Society of Journalists and Authors, among others.

Today FSB's primary focus is on online marketing, which includes designing author websites, working with authors on social media engagement strategies, and securing visibility for their work through online publicity.

For more information on FSB Associates, please visit www.FSBAssociates.com.

For more information about Fauzia Burke and this book, please visit www.FauziaBurke.com.

Berrett–Koehler
Publishers

Berrett-Koehler is an independent publisher dedicated to an ambitious mission: *connecting people and ideas to create a world that works for all.*

We believe that to truly create a better world, action is needed at all levels—individual, organizational, and societal. At the individual level, our publications help people align their lives with their values and with their aspirations for a better world. At the organizational level, our publications promote progressive leadership and management practices, socially responsible approaches to business, and humane and effective organizations. At the societal level, our publications advance social and economic justice, shared prosperity, sustainability, and new solutions to national and global issues.

A major theme of our publications is "Opening Up New Space." Berrett-Koehler titles challenge conventional thinking, introduce new ideas, and foster positive change. Their common quest is changing the underlying beliefs, mindsets, institutions, and structures that keep generating the same cycles of problems, no matter who our leaders are or what improvement programs we adopt.

We strive to practice what we preach—to operate our publishing company in line with the ideas in our books. At the core of our approach is stewardship, which we define as a deep sense of responsibility to administer the company for the benefit of all of our "stakeholder" groups: authors, customers, employees, investors, service providers, and the communities and environment around us.

We are grateful to the thousands of readers, authors, and other friends of the company who consider themselves to be part of the "BK Community." We hope that you, too, will join us in our mission.

A BK Life Book

This book is part of our BK Life series. BK Life books change people's lives. They help individuals improve their lives in ways that are beneficial for the families, organizations, communities, nations, and world in which they live and work. To find out more, visit **www.bk-life.com**.

Berrett–Koehler
Publishers

Connecting people and ideas
to create a world that works for all

Dear Reader,

Thank you for picking up this book and joining our worldwide community of Berrett-Koehler readers. We share ideas that bring positive change into people's lives, organizations, and society.

To welcome you, we'd like to offer you a free e-book. You can pick from among twelve of our bestselling books by entering the promotional code **BKP92E** here: http://www.bkconnection.com/welcome.

When you claim your free e-book, we'll also send you a copy of our e-newsletter, the *BK Communiqué*. Although you're free to unsubscribe, there are many benefits to sticking around. In every issue of our newsletter you'll find

- A free e-book
- Tips from famous authors
- Discounts on spotlight titles
- Hilarious insider publishing news
- A chance to win a prize for answering a riddle

Best of all, our readers tell us, "Your newsletter is the only one I actually read." So claim your gift today, and please stay in touch!

Sincerely,

Charlotte Ashlock
Steward of the BK Website

Questions? Comments? Contact me at bkcommunity@bkpub.com.

MIX
Paper from
responsible sources
FSC® C002589

Certified

Corporation
bcorporation.net